The
Essential
Guide to
Maui

Essential

Guide to

Maui

Many people assisted with this project, and it is impossible to name them all, but we would particularly like to thank the following, who were especially helpful:

Scott Stone; Kelli McCormack; Jeri Bostwick; Jean Brady, University of Hawai'i Press; Laureen Teixeira; Brooke Brown; Ruth Gurnani-Smith; Gwenda Iyechad; Julie King, Ted King, Kaanapali Windsurfing School; Rae and Linky Lindquist, Hotel Hana-Maui; Hawaiian Airlines; AB Makk; Gary Smith, Lahaina Galleries; Walelu Stone; Lisa Toomey; and Madge Tennent Walls.

Please address orders and
editorial correspondence to:

ISLAND HERITAGE PUBLISHING
A division of The Madden Corporation
99-880 Iwaena Street
Aiea, Hawai'i 96701
(808) 487-7299

THIRD EDITION, FIRST PRINTING — 1991
Printed in Hong Kong

Produced by:
THE MADDEN CORPORATION

Published by:
ISLAND HERITAGE PUBLISHING
A division of The Madden Corporation

1991 Editors:
PENNY PENCE SMITH
DIXON J. SMITH

Research Assistant:
LINDA S. TOUSSAINT

Art Direction/Production:
THE BAPTISTA GROUP

Page Layout/Photo Editor:
SCOTT RUTHERFORD

Cartography:
ANDREA HINES

Original Cover Artwork by:
MARK A. WAGENMAN
FEDERICK WOODRUFF

TABLE OF CONTENTS

INTRODUCTION

INTRODUCTION

Maui stands out as a brilliant, spectacularly diverse jewel in the strand of beautiful islands that make up Hawai'i. From the towering grandeur of the dormant volcano, Haleakalā, to the sweeping beaches of Kā'anapali, Maui truly fulfills the daydreamer's fantasy of what an idyllic tropical paradise should be. It is here that the visitor discovers both the charming, sleepy Hawaiian village of Hāna and the fast-paced resort center of West Maui. Bustling Lahaina, the center of the whaling industry of yesteryear and the capital of the whale-watching industry of today, reflects how Maui's rich past has evolved into a different, but no less fascinating, present. Maui commands a significant place in Hawai'i's colorful and occasionally turbulent history. Here, Hawaiian chiefs played out important stages in these islands' development.

GEOGRAPHY

Maui once was two islands, each with a volcanic peak soaring above the surface of the sea like tips of icebergs. Erosion wore down the flanks of the volcanoes until they connected in an isthmus, which Mauians today refer to as the Central Valley. Maui's commercial centers of Kahului and Wailuku are here. Other distinct regions are the old whaling port of Lahaina and West Maui; Kapalua, a sleepy tropical area at the far west of the island; the tropical areas of Kīhei and Mā'alaea along the southern coast; the Upcountry area, a place of lush pastures and cattle ranches on the slopes of Haleakalā; and, at the extreme east end, the lush, lovely Hāna.

Maui is the second largest island in Hawai'i, which consists of a string of islands in the North Pacific about a thousand miles from its nearest neighbors—the Line Islands to the south and the Marshall Islands to the southwest. Nothing but ocean lies between Hawai'i and southern California, 2390 miles [3846km] to the east-northeast; Japan, 3850 miles [6196km] to the west-northwest; and Alaska, 2600

miles [4184 km] to the north. The Marquesas—from which at least some of the early Polynesian migrants came—are 2400 miles [3862km] to the south-southeast.

The archipelago spans 1523 miles [2451km] and includes 132 islands, reefs and shoals strewn across the Tropic of Cancer—from Kure Atoll in the northwest to underwater seamounts off the coast of the island of Hawai'i in the southeast. All are included in the state of Hawai'i except the Midway Islands, which are administered by the US Navy. This southernmost part of the United States lies between latitudes 28° 15' and 18° 54'N and between longitudes 179° 25' and 154° 40'W, reaching almost as far west as Alaska's Aleutian Islands. Hawai'i's major islands share their tropical latitudes with such urban centers as Mexico City, Havana, Mecca, Calcutta, Hanoi and Hong Kong. The 158th meridian west, which passes through O'ahu's Pearl Harbor, also crosses Point Barrow on Alaska's north coast, Atiu Island in the South Pacific's Cook Islands and Cape Colbeck near the edge of Antarctica's Ross Ice Shelf.

Windsurfing at Ho'okipa Beach, the professionals' hangout.

4

While Hawai'i's land surface adds up to only 6425 square miles [16,642 sq km] (at that still larger than Connecticut, Delaware or Rhode Island), the archipelago, including its territorial waters, covers a total of about 654,500 square miles [1,695,155 sq km]—an area considerably bigger than Alaska and more than twice the size of Texas.

Maui is one of eight main islands in the Hawaiian chain. Kaho'olawe is used for target practice by the military, and is not inhabited. The tiny island of Ni'ihau is privately owned and can be visited by non-residents only at the invitation of its owners—an honor rarely bestowed on anyone. This island—due to its fierce protection from outside influence—is the last stronghold of Hawaiian culture (its entire population [226] is of at least part-Hawaiian blood), and it is the only place on the planet where Hawaiian is still spoken as the mother tongue. Scenic helicopter flights over the island may touch down for up to twenty minutes, but no contact with the residents is permitted.

That leaves visitors to Hawai'i the islands of Kaua'i, O'ahu, Moloka'i, Lāna'i, Maui, and Hawai'i (familiarly known as 'the Big Island')—in that order, north to south and chronologically in age—to explore.

HISTORY

More than two centuries ago King Kahekili ruled all of Maui except for the Hāna area, which fell under the de facto control of Kalaniopu'u, a powerful ruler on the island of Hawai'i to the south. In 1776, Kalaniopu'u's armies invaded Maui, but Kahekili's warriors annihilated them in a famous battle near Wailuku. Kahekili, justly famous as a mighty king in his own right, also may have been the father of Kamehameha, destined to unite all the islands in his kingdom.

In 1786 a French expedition led by Captain Jean Francois de Galaup, Comte de La Perouse, anchored in a sheltered bay south of Wailea and Mākena. The next day, La Perouse became the first non-Hawaiian to set foot on Maui. (Cook had seen Maui, but sailed by after failing to quickly find an anchorage.) Maui soon became a regular port of call.

Four years after La Perouse's arrival, Kamehameha's forces defeated the army of Kahekili, and Kamehameha, who became known as the 'Napoleon of the Pacific', brought Maui under his control. In 1793, Captain Vancouver sailed into Lahaina and confirmed La Perouse's earlier report of a fine anchorage. In less than a dozen years, Kamehameha's 'Pelelu Fleet' of canoes lingered on West Maui beaches before he sailed on to conquer O'ahu. The first whaling vessel, *The Balaena*, stopped off in Lahaina in 1819 and was a harbinger of the vast fleets to come.

Of more lasting impact, Christians built their first mission in Lahaina in 1823, and the great conversion of Maui—and Hawai'i—gained impetus. At the same time, the standard of education on the island improved, attracting the children of the rich from other islands and even the US mainland. With the decline of whaling,

George Wilfong started the first sugar plantation on Maui in 1849 in Hāna. A dozen years later James Campbell built the first great sugar mill on the island. By 1900 more than half the population on Maui were Chinese and Japanese citizens working the eleven sugar plantation fields. Through the efforts of such men as Henry Perrine Baldwin and Samuel Thomas Alexander, the sugar industry gained preeminence. Claus Spreckels had large holdings on Maui, and built an enormous irrigation ditch that brought fifty million gallons of water a day from Hā'iku (Upcountry) to the area of Pu'unēnē (Central Valley) so that sugar could prosper. Maui's center of focus shifted from Lahaina to Pā'ia, a sugar town with a nearby mill.

Not far away, near the governmental seat at Wailuku, the port of Kahului developed into the island's principal seaport; it also was headquarters for a prosperous railroad operation, with narrow-gauge passenger and freight trains underway between Wailuku-Kahului and Spreckelsville-Pā'ia.

By 1930 transportation on Maui, and between islands, had improved considerably. There were some 5000 'gas-driven cars' on Maui streets and roads. Inter-Island Airways, Ltd., landed its first Sikorsky aircraft on Maui in 1929 and began regular service from the airport at Mā'alaea.

Like the rest of Hawai'i, Maui was shocked by the attack on Pearl Harbor on December 7, 1941. Maui contributed manpower to the war effort and bought more than its share of war bonds.

Post-war Maui took part in the gradual, then rapid, development of the islands. With its stunning scenery, its splendid beaches and lush pastures, and perhaps the best climate of all the islands, Maui began to attract visitors who wanted more from Hawai'i than the comparatively urban, fast-paced atmosphere of Waikīkī and the rest of O'ahu. Suddenly, Maui sparkled with a new vitality that continues today.

Watching the sunset from Haleakalā can be an almost spiritual experience.

CULTURAL BACKGROUND

In anonymity and out of Asia, the ancestors of the Hawaiians began millenia ago to work their way across the vast, trackless Pacific. They journeyed from Central Asia to southeast Asia, poised on the brink of a great adventure: the people of the land were about to become the people of the sea, and ultimately the people of 'many islands', for that is what the word Polynesia means. As they moved, they changed, altering their gods to the demands of new places, subtly reworking their myths and legends and genealogies to make them compatible with the enormous seas and the evolution of their canoes. Their mode of dress changed; their physical statures altered as they adapted to life on, and in, the water.

At some point in these long and epic voyages, the Polynesians stood offshore in the lee of a group of islands at the apex of a triangle formed by New Zealand, Tahiti and Hawai'i. Some nameless Polynesian sailor, more than eleven centuries ago, shouted excitedly to the rest of the crew and pointed out islands that would mark the crowning achievement of the long voyages. That sailor and the rest of the crew are believed today to have been from the Marquesas island group far to the southeast.

More voyages back and forth followed. One day, a new group of energetic islanders, the Polynesians

A laid-back afternoon on the Hāna Coast.

from Tahiti, made the journey. In all likelihood there was war. Or perhaps it was merely the dominance of a strong, aggressive race. Whatever the cause, by about AD 1100, the people from Tahiti had surfaced as the unquestioned masters in a magnificent new home. They gave it a name: Hawai'i. Later, some would say the name had no significance, while others believed it was a variation of Hawaiki, the legendary homeland of all Polynesians.

Other newcomers made landfall here over the centuries. Seeds came in the bellies of birds; coconuts washed ashore on the beaches, and took hold. Wind-blown pollen and insects bumped up against the islands' high mountains. Natural springs and rivers formed.

The Polynesians added variety to the indigenous plants, introducing bananas, coconuts, sweet potatoes, bamboo, ginger, yams, breadfruit and candlenut [kukui] tree. They also brought dogs, chickens and pigs to Hawai'i. In time, a new civilization developed as the settlers became less Polynesian and more Hawaiian.

The life of the average Hawaiian was ordered, and he was often powerless to change it. The ali'i, the royalty, were absolute masters. A second group, the kāhuna, or priests, cast a long shadow and dealt in both the natural and supernatural. As kāhuna, the priests were known to talk with the gods and interpret signs, and were not adverse to using their powers. The ordinary men and women were maka'ainana, in many

Heading down Haleakalā Highway, with Upcountry's green pastures below.

cases born to a time and place that locked them into a pattern from which they could not escape.

But it was not altogether a grim life. The *maka'ainana* lived in a healthy, uncrowded and stunningly beautiful archipelago where they arose to brilliant mornings and retired awash in sunsets of great beauty. They had their *makahiki*, or traditional games, and they revered their old people, the *kūpuna*. They cared about the family unit and about their *'ohana*, or extended family. By the time Westerners arrived here, the Hawaiian society had become complex, colorful and

lives of the Hawaiians.

The islands impressed Cook, who was surprised to find that the inhabitants spoke a variation of the languages he had heard earlier in the South Pacific. He wrote of the natives' generosity and worried over their tendency to steal; he watched with both understanding and dismay as the native girls, the *wāhine*, came aboard his two ships. He knew such liaisons with his men were inevitable, but he also knew some of his sailors were infected with venereal disease.

Cook, revered as the god Lono, was killed by Hawaiians on the

Camping in Haleakalā National Park near the ocean.

yet infused with this strict sense of order.

The great English explorer and navigator, Captain James Cook, found these lonely North Pacific islands on January 18, 1778. European diseases and Western weapons followed, dramatically changing the

beach at Kealakekua, on the southernmost island, after a misunderstanding. Had he lived he would have seen the diseases decimate the Hawaiian population from 300,000 in 1778 to fewer than 50,000 a century later. And by 1878, other forces had diminished the influence of the Hawaiians in their own land.

In Kamehameha's lifetime, Hawaiian power reached its zenith. Tough and energetic, intelligent and implacable, Kamehameha had inherited the war god Kuka'ilimoku from his uncle, Kalaniopu'u, ranking chief at Kealakekua. He also inherited a tall frame and a tactician's approach to problem-solving. When Kamehameha saw the superior firepower of European guns and the logic of European tactics in war, he immediately appropriated English advisors and set out to buy guns. He wanted to become the person who linked the islands, each under one or more chieftains, into a true kingdom with himself at its head. By craft and treachery, by bravery and a modicum of luck, Kamehameha fulfilled his dream. A series of bloody wars and a bit of diplomacy with the king of Kaua'i brought all the islands under his rule.

Under Kamehameha there was extensive trade and interaction with the West. When he allowed, ships from abroad filled Hawaiian harbors; but he also was careful to maintain the old ways among his people. The *kapu* system that allowed the *ali'i* to lay an edict over any person, place or thing remained in effect until Kamehameha died. If the Hawaiians did not fully understand the concept of nationhood, they certainly understood the power of authority. Kamehameha ruled as much by force of personality as by force of arms.

Upon his death on May 8, 1819, at the end of years of peace and stability, Kamehameha was buried in a secret place. It is a secret that endures. Today, no one knows the burial site of the greatest of all Hawaiians.

Almost immediately Kamehameha's influence began to dissipate. A week after the king's death, his favorite wife, Ka'ahumanu, declared Kamehameha's son, Liholiho, the next ruler; but, she added, she would rule with him. In time she pressured Liholiho into abandoning the *kapu* system, and the inevitable change followed.

About the time Kamehameha died, word flashed around the maritime nations that there were enormous herds of whales in the Pacific. The news galvanized seamen who knew the Atlantic grounds held fewer and fewer whales, and Hawai'i assumed a new importance.

Within three years, up to sixty whaling ships at a time anchored in Honolulu Harbor alone, and the waters off Lahaina were dark with the timbers of ships. Sailors came to rely on Hawai'i's ports for girls, grog and stores. There was, they said, "no God west of the Horn," and they seemed bent on proving it. Whaling became an important industry to Hawai'i; whalingmen became a prime nuisance.

Whaling meant money. Goods were transshipped, ships were repaired, and the activity attracted non-whaling merchant vessels as well.

Whaling also bewildered and confused the *maka'āinana*, who saw the sailors indulging themselves without punishment. By now the Hawaiians had no strong system of their own to turn to for strength, and they were finding it difficult to make sense of their lives and times.

A second group of foreigners, or *haole*, confused Hawaiians more than a little. The missionaries had arrived in 1819, with their stern visages and rigid lifestyles, their talk of Trinity and damnation. Between the whalers and the missionaries, battles raged over the land and souls of the native Hawaiians.

In their way the missionaries turned out to be as tough as the oak planking of the whaling ships. Arriving first on the brig *Thaddeus* on October 23, 1819, the missionaries found the Hawaiian society in chaos following Kamehameha's death. They also found a dearth of new ideas, and moved quickly to fill the vacuum. Liholiho came to be regarded as a friend. The missionaries converted Keōpūolani, the queen mother, then the powerful chieftess Kapi'olani. Within two years the missionaries standardized the written form of Hawaiian, printed bibles and opened schools. They became a powerful force in the islands, and their descendants would become leaders of Hawai'i society, business and industry.

Hawai'i attracted more and more foreigners. Americans, Britons, French, Germans and Scots traveled to Hawai'i, drawn to the image of a tropical paradise, held by the opportunities they found.

In 1859 an oil well went into production in Pennsylvania, signaling the end of the whaling industry. Whales no longer were the only source of the oil for which they were slaughtered. War broke out between the Union and the Confederacy, and many whaling ships were pressed into service as merchantmen, decreasing markedly the whaling fleet. Finally, in the fall of 1871, ice caught thirty-three whaling ships in Arctic waters north of the Bering Strait and remorselessly crushed the last hope of a viable whaling industry.

In Hawai'i, new industries

flourished, one of them sugar. Planters needed cheap agricultural labor, and had to look to foreign countries because diseases had vastly reduced the Hawaiian population. Plantation owners turned first to China, then to Japan, then to Portugal, the Philippines and other places. This marked the beginning of Hawai'i's melting pot. Land ownership, which before Cook's arrival was reserved only for the *ali'i*, became an increasingly perplexing problem. The Hawaiian government gave up rights to all property except certain lands for the king. Commoners now were permitted to buy land, and foreigners could lease it. The *haole*, having come from civilizations that prized land ownership, reached for as much as they could get. The average Hawaiian, at sea with all the attendant bureaucracy, just got more confused. On the one hand he could lease or cultivate his land, rights he never before possessed. On the other hand, it became easy to sell it to the *haole*. The Great Mahele, the movement that began with attempts to tie the Hawaiians closer to their land, ended in them losing it in great quantities.

In the 1890s, conflicts grew between Queen Lili'uokalani, destined to be the last Hawaiian monarch, and a group of businessmen who objected to the queen's push for a new constitution that would have restored much of the Hawaiian royalty's lost powers. On January 17, 1893, the monarchy toppled, and the Republic of Hawai'i formed—with a new constitution.

Five years later, on August 12, 1898, spectators jammed the area around 'Iolani Palace in Honolulu to hear the Hawaiian national anthem

The largest Buddha outside of Asia sits at the Lahaina Jodo Mission.

played and watch the Hawaiian flag slowly lowered to the ground. The American flag was raised in its place; the American national anthem was played; and Sanford Ballard Dole, a leader in the monarchy's overthrow, was sworn in as first chief executive officer of the Territory of Hawai'i, a US possession.

Stability and social change followed. The melting pot became more so, and a lifestyle emerged in which racial groups were proud of their ancestry, but also proud of their Americanization. It seemed, there was a little Hawaiian blood in almost everybody. For more than four decades, the largely agricul-

tural community went about its business, attracted a few visitors, and never dreamed it would be the target of a sudden attack that became the impetus for the US to enter World War II.

On Sunday, December 7, 1941, Japanese aircraft swarmed in from a fleet that had crept unseen and unheard across the Pacific to a point north of the islands. The devastating raid on Pearl Harbor plunged the US into the war and brought quick changes to Hawai'i. Martial law was declared, a military government installed in 'Iolani Palace, and thousands of young US servicemen turned up in the islands. Some never left. Intermarriages soared. By the end of the war the whole fabric of Hawai'i society had changed with the interweaving of the new *haole* immigrants. The end of the war also saw the return of the young *Nisei*—the second generation Japanese— who thirsted for political power and determined to put an end to the long rule of the entrenched Republican establishment of the day.

With their GI Bill for Education, the veterans went off to colleges and came back as lawyers, doctors, accountants and other professionals. They were politically oriented and hard-working, and they swept up with them other young men

Pineapple fields in Pukalani.

in Hawai'i fired by ambition. In 1954, in a thunderous victory, the veterans took over the top positions in Hawai'i and forced a new, political equality on the Establishment. In another five years, statehood marked the beginning of still another era of change.

Statehood meant stability for investments; the invention of the jet meant an influx of tourists; and international publicity about America's newest state turned Hawai'i into a magnet for those seeking a new life in a paradisical setting. Tourism edged out agriculture as the primary source of revenue, which it remains to this day. Visitor industry revenues account for a third of all local taxes, and exceed sugar and pineapple revenues combined. More than a third of the local labor force have jobs in the visitor industry.

THE ENVIRONMENT

Fairly recently in the history of the Earth—only 25 million years ago—a series of cracks opened northwest to southeast in the ocean floor of the North Pacific. In tumultuous explosions followed by

An artist captures Lahaina Harbor's ethereal sunset tones.

fiery rivers of magma, molten lava, land began to build up underneath the surface of the sea.

In time, the land broke the surface and lay barren and exposed to winds and the pounding sea. The rise and fall of ice caps thousands of miles away helped raise or lower the level of the sea. Still the land remained, buffeted by winds, clawed by seas which broke over the exposed shoreline. Then there was a time of quiet.

In a thundering end to the silence, the lava explosions began again. Lava flows tumbled and rolled down the sides of the mountains and, in astonishing pyrotechnics, more land was born. As the land increased, so did its diversity, as wind and waves continued to carve coves and valleys. Algae and coral polyps began to build reefs around the land. With the seeding of the land by birds, drifting coconuts and other material, the land began to turn green.

When the Polynesians arrived they brought their own versions of how the land came to be. In one account, a mischievous Polynesian demigod called Māui fished the land up from the bottom of the ocean. A myth common to much of Polynesia held that the islands were the children of gods, usually Papa and Wakea, earth-mother and sky-father.

Today the islands are but the tops of volcanic mountains, enormous when measured from the ocean floor up. They lie like beads on a string across the 1523 miles of ocean, and are made up almost entirely of lava.

Abundant, high-quality water and clean air bless this environ-mental wonderland. Plant life in Hawai'i also is a naturalist's dream. More than 2500 kinds of plants grow only in Hawai'i. Because of Hawai'i's long isolation, evolution of plant life has been rapid and diverse. Conversely, plants that are found throughout the Pacific were not present in Hawai'i until man brought them—such as the banyan, taro and figs. Most of the myriad orchids that grace Hawai'i today came from other places. There is only one native palm tree.

Because Hawai'i is so far from other land, very few animals arrived here under their own power. The hoary bat (Lasiurus) is an exception. The Hawaiian bat is smaller than its distant relatives but tough enough to fly long distances. The Hawaiian monk seal (Monachus), a species related to seals in the Caribbean and the Mediterranean, also arrived from afar. It may have been the first mammal to live in Hawai'i, and today is found nowhere else. The Polynesian rat (Rattus) stowed away aboard Polynesian voyaging canoes, and, like the Polynesians them-selves, originated in Asia. The Polynesians valued the domestic dog (Canis) as a pet, food source and a part of religious rituals. By all accounts the Polynesian dog was highly dependent and unaggressive, and as new breeds of dogs came to the islands, the original version disappeared.

The presence of pigs (Sus scrofa) in the islands turned out to be a mixed blessing. They were an important food source, but when they began to run wild in the lush forests they became a nuisance, and more. Today feral pigs are blamed for destroying much of the islands' watershed areas by digging up the

Gentle surf washes along Kīhei's sandy shores.

forest floor and the aquifer, the natural filter through which a lot of island water flows.

Captain Cook released goats in Hawai'i, and others who came after him brought sheep, cattle and horses. These large animals were extremely destructive to Hawaiian plants. By 1900 many native plants below roughly 1200 feet had been eradicated, some replaced by heartier species. Today these large animals are an asset, not a menace.

Hawai'i's isolation also gave rise to a unique bird life. Today, however, more than half the birds the US government lists as rare or endangered are birds of Hawai'i. More than four times as many birds have become extinct in Hawai'i as in the entire North American continent. The birds succumbed to hunters, introduced predators, the swift mongooses brought to Hawai'i, combat rats and urban encroachment.

Many birds live near streams, marshes or ponds; the largest number inhabit the deep forests. Perhaps the most dramatic are the long-winged seabirds. Twenty-two different species spend their non-breeding time flying over the open ocean, scavenging for food and resting on the water, coming back to Hawai'i to breed. Millions of them nest in the sanctuary of uninhabited small islands northwest of the occupied islands of Hawai'i. Some birds that were introduced to the islands from elsewhere and thrive here include pigeons, doves, mynas, cardinals and sparrows. The state bird is the nēnē (Branta sandvicensis), a goose that lives high on the rugged slopes of the volcanoes. The nēnē has battled back from near-extinction. Many of Hawai'i's birds

are found only on specific islands, such as the 'io, or hawk (Buteo solitarius), found only on the island of Hawai'i.

Long before any land mammals came—and before plants, or even birds—marine mammals swam the surrounding seas. In fact, the ancestors of some of the whales and dolphins now found in Hawaiian waters may have been here even before the islands arose from the sea. They include the humpback whales, which today are seasonal visitors, several varieties of dolphins, killer whales, sperm whales—in all, at least twenty types. Today the most popular marine mammal is the humpback whale, important enough to Maui to deserve singling out for special attention (see The Whales on next page).

Other marine life became important to the Hawaiians, not only for food but in rituals, legends, myths and mele [chants]. Hawaiian fishermen had their own god, Ku'ulakai, and small fishing shrines [ko'a] were dedicated near water to the god. The shrines often were no more than stacked rocks, but they were significant to the fishermen who offered the first of their catch at the ko'a.

Certain fish were considered tastier than others; fishermen often offered red and white fish to the gods. Some Hawaiian families considered certain fish, particularly sharks, to be their 'aumakua or household god.

Each wave of newcomer brought its own fishing mystique, taste and style. Today the fishing practices of Hawai'i's people reflect the state's multi-racial populace and preserve the islands' reputation as a top marine science center.

THE WHALES

Each year the humpback whales come to Maui, seeking waters that are about 75° F [24° C] and the shelter of the leeward shores and quiet bays. They come down from the Arctic to Hawaiian waters to breed, generally from October to May. They cover some 2800 miles in an estimated eighty to a hundred days, and while in Hawaiian waters, they fast.

They do not arrive in herds, but flow in and out of the breeding grounds through the winter months, some staying as late as July. The newly pregnant females leave first for northern waters, followed by younger whales and then the more mature of both sexes.

Intelligence, size, gentleness—all have endeared the humpback whales to the people of Maui, who have been in the forefront of efforts to protect the whales. Not until recently did man pay much atten-tion to the whales' sensitivity and intelligence. They have a communi-cations system that produces sounds of haunting beauty—and specific intent. Whales also have a highly developed sense of direction and good eyesight, both in water and air (they are known to surface to look at passing ships).

Calves not only are conceived in Hawaiian waters; many are born here. Mother whales give birth in relatively shallow water of about 150 feet to discourage predators, and produce up to 130 gallons of milk a day for their offspring.

The whales' annual journey here allows the visitor to Maui an opportunity to see these massive ocean creatures at fairly close range—an experience possible in relatively few other places in the world. For more information on the humpback whale and whale watching see SPORTS.

CLIMATE and WEATHER

Maui's pleasant climate doesn't change much throughout the year—at sea level. The temperature ranges between a daytime high near 90° F [about 30° C] in 'summer' and a nighttime low near 60° F [about 18° C] in 'winter'. There really are no distinct seasons as such. Even in 'winter' the daytime temperature is usually in the 80s. The comfort factor that this involves depends on what you're used to: where you've come from and how long you've been here. People do acclimatize. Those of us who live here start to shiver and bundle up when the mercury plummets to 75° F [24° C]. The coldest months are February and March and the hottest August and September.

Despite this lack of strong seasonal variation, Hawai'i is home to an extraordinary diversity of microclimates—from desert to rainforest. Temperature drops about 3° F for every thousand feet of increased altitude, a factor which has produced seasonal snow on the upper slopes of Haleakalā. Rainfall varies dramatically in different parts of each island. All this lush tropical foliage requires a lot of rain, yet drought in some areas of the Islands is not unheard-of. The State's heaviest rains are brought by storms between October and April. Most local rainshowers are short if heavy, except in the upper reaches of valleys where the rainclouds never leave for long. The windward areas get far more rain than their leeward counterparts.

There have been few damaging storms or tsunami (seismic sea waves) in Hawai'i. Hurricane Iwa, active in 1982, brought gusts of 100 miles per hour and caused an estimated $234 million in losses.

TIME and DAYLIGHT

Because of Hawai'i's tropical location, the length of daylight doesn't vary greatly from one time of year to the next—only about three or four hours—so that Hawai'i residents have never felt any need to save it. Thus Hawaiian Standard Time is in effect year-round, and the time difference between Hawai'i and places that do save daylight varies by an hour when daylight saving is in effect elsewhere.

Hawaiian Standard Time is five hours behind New York, four hours behind Chicago, three hours behind Denver and two hours behind San Francisco; it is also eleven hours behind London, nineteen hours behind Tokyo, twenty hours behind Sydney, and twenty-two hours behind Auckland and Suva. Add an hour to all these for daylight time. The popular local phrase 'Hawaiian time' simply means 'late'.

THE FLAG

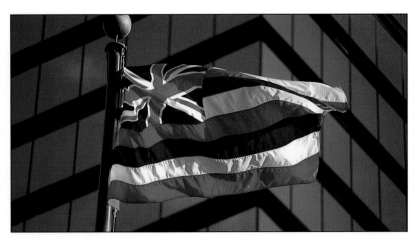

The British Union Jack in the corner of Hawai'i's State flag intrigues most first-time visitors to Hawai'i. This same flag has served Kingdom, Republic and State and was designed prior to 1816 for King Kamehameha I. The Union Jack

honors Hawai'i's early ties with Britain; the eight horizontal stripes represent the archipelago's eight main islands. Hawai'i's State Anthem, 'Hawai'i Pono'ī', is its former national anthem and was composed by King Kalākaua.

LANGUAGE

English became the common language of Hawaiian commerce very early in the era of immigration and economic investment by Americans and other foreigners. And so it remained. The missionaries made sweeping and now irreversible changes in the Hawaiian language when they hurriedly transliterated and transcribed it for print in order to produce bibles. Subsequent efforts to stamp out the native tongue were very successful. There are only a several hundred native speakers left—most either very old or from the private island of Ni'ihau. A strong grassroots movement to save the language has taken hold in recent years and is gaining widespread support. Virtually everyone in the islands today speaks the American variety of English, with a few local variations on the theme. Some of these should be noted because they are so common. Perhaps most important is the local way of giving directions. Nobody ever uses the cardinal points of the compass. On an island these are far less relevant than the obvious 'toward the mountain' and 'toward the sea'. A contracted form of the Hawaiian words for these directions is universally used in

Mauians give their friendly 'shaka' signs.

Hawai'i. 'Toward the mountain [uka]' is mauka; 'toward the sea [kai]' is makai.

The other major obstacle, for some, to comfortably getting around is the ubiquitous use of Hawaiian placenames and streetnames. The Hawaiian language is beautiful and only looks intimidating to non-Polynesians because they are not accustomed to seeing so many vowels in a row. **Basically, if you just pronounce all the letters one by one, you'll be fine.** In fact you might, at that, be pronouncing Hawaiian more correctly than a lot of people who are used to it. The 'glottal stop' (written ') is the hard sound created by stopping between vowel sounds, like the English 'oh-oh', rather than a sliding from one vowel to the next, as is usual. In Hawaiian, this is called 'okina. Just stop talking then start again immediately. The macron (written as a - over a vowel), called kahakō in Hawaiian, simply means that vowel is held a little longer—as if it were written twice, which it occasionally is. Consonants are pronounced the same as in English except that w sounds like v when it immediately precedes a final single vowel and occasionally at other times. Vowels are pronounced as in Spanish or Italian (ah, eh, ee, oh, oo). The vowel combinations ai, ae, ao, au, ei, eu, oi and ou are stressed on the first member and basically sounded as single units, though the second vowel in the set is truly pronounced

and not lost in the combination as with English diphthongs. Otherwise, stress (accent) is almost always on the next-to-last syllable. No matter how many times you hear it along the tourist trail, the very special and wonderfully soft Hawaiian word aloha is NOT correctly pronounced with the stress on the last syllable.

You will often see Hawaiian words written without the kahakō and 'okina. This was the custom of the English-speaking people who first transcribed the language and was common practice until fairly recently. The markings are necessary for correct pronunciation of many words, and for discerning between similarly spelt words with quite different meanings. Government policy is now to insert the correct markings in all Hawaiian words on street and road signs as they are replaced.

The other feature of local language that visitors are bound to encounter is our own brand of pidgin English. It is spiced with words from the rich linguistic heritage brought by people of many lands, but basically, it is English with a bit of Hawaiian. If you listen carefully, you'll catch on. The idiom and the lilt are peculiar to Hawai'i, but the pronunciation of most words is quite recognizable.

Lists of commonly used Hawaiian and pidgin words with their meanings and pronunciations can be found at the back of this book.

IN TRANSIT

GETTING HERE

Y ou've daydreamed about your journey to Maui, and weaved scenarios in your mind about your vacation in this breathtakingly beautiful place. Now you are ready to take some of the practical steps that will make this visit as exciting and pleasurable as your dreams. Making those arrangements is easy and not all that expensive. This section spells out the options to choose from to tailor your trip to your specifications. Most people choose to travel by air rather than sea, though the latter is still possible, and most arrive during the winter season, with February at peak, and in August.

CHOOSING LOCATION

Exquisite beaches fringe the lovely island of Maui, so it is not surprising that most hotels and condominiums are on or near the beach. Here is a brief summary of the various areas of Maui to help you decide where to visit:

Kā'anapali—A man-made resort on a beach nature perfected, Kā'anapali is a world-class destination area in West Maui with resort hotels and all the attendant amenities.

There are, literally, thousands of hotel rooms in this area, and several condominiums in nearby Lahaina, the historic old whaling town.

Kapalua—Here is another resort carved out of lava and scrub brush on the edge of a gorgeous beach. This resort hotel area north of Kā'anapali features luxurious amenities. Between here and Kā'anapali, numerous condominiums of varying price ranges provide

Following Sliding Sands Trail in Haleakalā Crater on horseback.

a beach-goer's haven.

Kīhei/Wailea/Mākena—Condominiums abound along the sunny southern coast, and are located either on the beach or close by. The condominiums give way to some of Maui's most stunning hotels along pristine beaches at the resort area of Wailea. Farther south, the beautiful beaches of Mākena contribute to Maui's idyllic reputation, but there are few accommodations in this area. However, the beaches are within easy striking distance from any condominium in Kīhei. A new first-class hotel, the Maui Prince, graces a fine beach at Mākena.

Hāna—This area on the far eastern tip of Maui offers the best of both worlds: there are beautiful beaches on the shoreline, and above is an adjoining cattle ranch with Haleakalā towering in the background. Again, accommodations in this area are relatively limited, but advance planning can get you a hotel room, a condominium or even a cabin for a limited time.

Upcountry Maui—On the slopes of Haleakalā, the nights are cool, the mornings crisp and the views outstanding. Here is where you'll smell smoke from fireplaces on winter mornings, and walk among hardwood forests. There are limited visitor accommodations in this area, and if you won't mind being located away from the beach, this is a wonderful alternative.

Central Valley—The Wailuku-Kahului area has few beaches, but it does provide history and character for the visitor who prefers to be out of the tourist mainstream and into the heart of an unfamiliar place. Wailuku is the capital of the island, the seat of government, and a charming old town that is taking its restoration seriously. It is home to a number of historic sites as well as the intriguing 'Iao Valley Park and 'Iao Needle.

A family walk along Wailea Beach in the mild afternoon sun.

SELECTING LODGING

Those who wish to be pampered during their Maui vacation choose to stay in hotels, many of which are near the heart of the action, and where friendly, efficient staffs cater to the needs of guests. Other visitors—especially those traveling with children—prefer the self-contained apartments available at condominium resorts. This option usually is less expensive and offers more privacy and independence. Bed-and-breakfast accommodation in private homes is an increasingly popular option for budget-minded travelers and for those wishing to avoid crowds, and exclusive use of private homes also is available for longer-term visits. The latter option is popular with families visiting during the summer months. Another family favorite is camping, either in rustic rural cabins or in tents. Specific places that offer these various types of lodging are described in detail under ACCOMMODATION.

WHAT TO BRING

Visitors should pack warm-weather clothing to wear in this perpetual spring and summer climate. Appropriate attire is casual. Shorts are acceptable almost anywhere, though many businesses require customers to wear shoes (rubber thongs will usually suffice). Comfortable walking shoes are a must. Sleeveless or short-sleeved shirts usually are best for the day, but long sleeves—or even a jacket or sweater—may be needed for cool winter evenings and air-conditioned buildings. A few deluxe restaurants and nightclubs have a dress code requiring men to wear jackets, though usually not ties.

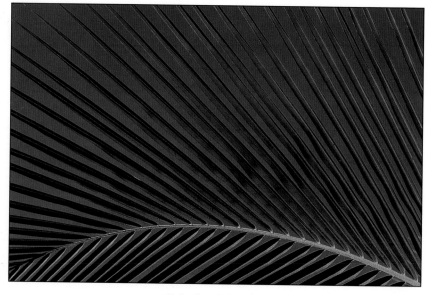

Palm frond close-up.

PERMITS and LICENSES

Some activities, such as driving and camping, require licenses or permits. Any visitor who drives in Maui must have a valid driver's license from another state or a Canadian province or a current international driver's license issued in another country.

Camping permits are required for public parks that allow camping, detailed in the Camping and Cabins subsection under ACCOMMODA-TION.

All hunting requires a license, as does freshwater fishing; none is required for recreational ocean or shore fishing. Further details of these sporting licenses are discussed under relevant headings in the SPORTS section.

No vaccinations or inoculations are required for entry into Hawai'i.

BOOKINGS

To reserve air or cruise tickets, lodging, and any tours you would like to take while visiting Maui, consult your travel agent.

You could spend days chasing specifics and comparing prices, and you may want to, but travel agents have most of the information you are likely to need at their fingertips. They know their sources well. It costs you no more, as an agent's commission is paid by the provider, not the customer; and in many cases the agent can offer you a better deal than you could get if you booked directly because agents shave their profit and pass that savings on to you.

Many airlines and hotels also give priority to bookings made through agents as they are generally less likely to be canceled.

Airlines

Most airlines fly directly to Honolulu, where passengers may switch to interisland aircraft to continue their journey; the additional trip usually averages twenty minutes. However, some airlines fly directly into Maui's Kahului Airport nonstop from the US mainland. They are **United Airlines, American Airlines** and **Delta Airlines**.

Most airlines that serve the Hawaiian Islands land at Honolulu International Airport. Airfares are relatively inexpensive because of the many flights and stiff competition for passengers. Flight times are roughly five hours from California, nine hours from Chicago, eleven hours from New York, eight hours from Tokyo and nine and a half hours from Sydney. Domestic carriers providing service to and from the US mainland are **America West, American Airlines, Continental, Delta, Garuda Indonesia, Hawaiian Airlines, Northwest Airlines, Pan Am, TWA** and **United Airlines**. Foreign carriers currently serving Honolulu are **Air New Zealand, Canadian Airlines International, China Airlines, Japan Air Lines, Korean Air, Philippine Airlines, Qantas** and **Singapore Airlines**. Please note, however, that these lists are subject to change without notice. Your travel agent will have all the latest details and schedules. Interisland carriers servicing Maui's airports are **Air Molokai** (800-262-6055, 521-0090), **Aloha Airlines** (244-9071), **Aloha IslandAir** (800 652-6541), **Hawaiian Airlines** (244-9111), and **Panorama Air** (836-2122, mainland: 800-367-2671, inter-island: 800-352-3732).

Cruise lines

Traveling to Hawai'i by cruise ship is far more complicated now than it was decades ago when many of our visitors sailed in to our island ports. Today, most of the cruise lines that stop here—**P & O Lines,**

Horseback riding in Hāna's lush pastures alongside crashing surf.

Princess Cruises, Royal Viking Line, Cunard Line and other European-based cruise operators— are of foreign registry and are forbidden by US law from transporting American citizens from one US port to another US port. This law—the Jones Act—was passed in 1896. Thus, if you board a foreign vessel in New York or California, you may visit Hawai'i, but cannot make it or any other US port your final destination. You may, if you board ship in another country, make Hawai'i or another American port your final destination, but most cruise operators today don't encourage one-way traffic. Still, it is possible, and there really is no more beautiful way to arrive here than by sea.

American Hawaii Cruises has two ships, the SS *Constitution* and SS *Independence*, that cruise the Hawaiian island chain on a weekly basis. They make a few trips a year to the ports of Seattle, San Francisco and Los Angeles.

If your dream is to come here by ship, your travel agent will be able to provide dates of upcoming transPacific voyages by these US-registered vessels, or contact American Hawaii Cruises (800 227-3666). For details of interisland cruises, see GETTING AROUND.

27

An ocean liner and container ship at port in Kahului.

Tours

Maui offers such a large assortment of tours and tour operators, that a list of them and their continually changing fees and schedules would be immmediately outdated. Your travel agent will be able to book tours for you through the larger companies, if you want your trip precisely planned.

Many visitors, though, who like the flexibility and spontaniety, prefer to book tours after arrival and a bit of scouting around. A selection of sightseeing tours and tour companies are described under GETTING AROUND.

MAUI AIRPORTS

Maui's principal airport is Kahului, located in the Central Valley. More than a hundred flights a day in addition to helicopter traffic and the occasional private jet land there. The airport is a full-service complex with lockers, information booth, car rental agencies and taxi service. A seventy plus million dollar expansion project that will add more amenities and conveniences to the airport is already partially finished.

The Kapalua-West Maui Airport, opened for service to commuter airlines in 1987, now has a snack shop, gift shop, lei/flower shop, porter service, and a free shuttle service, the Kā'anapali Trolley, between the airport and nearby Kā'anapali resort hotels. The service is scheduled every fifteen minutes. At the airport are three car rental agencies, Budget, Dollar, and Hertz. Hawaiian Airlines services this airport and can be telephoned there directly (669-4866). Princeville Airways (669-0255) also can be telephoned there for scheduling.

Hāna's airport is little more than a landing strip, with no amenities. However, pickup service is available through Hotel Hana-Maui (248-8211) if you are a hotel guest.

Play—the primary objective for everyone at Kā'anapali Beach.

HONOLULU AIRPORT

Serving as gateway between East and West and to all the outer islands, this is one of the busiest airports in the world. Passengers arriving from the US mainland or from other countries emerge from the catacombs of this vast complex on the ground level of the main terminal building. The airport's second level services Mainland and overseas departures and includes ticket counters for reservations and check-in, monitors with departure information, and all departure gates.

Most arriving and departing interisland flights service passengers from the interisland terminal, located next to the main terminal building at the westward end.

GETTING AROUND

N o single road connects all the areas that make up this wonderfully diverse island. For example, the northern seacoast area is passable in four-wheel-drive vehicles, but should not be attempted in anything else. When planning tours or simply driving and sightseeing, it is important to remember that Maui falls easily into distinct regions: West Maui, with its exceptional climate, magnificent beaches, the old whaling town of Lahaina and the resort area of Kā'anapali, is the region most visitors know best. Kapalua, at the far western end of Maui, boasts an elegant resort area and stunning beach. The southern shore from Mā'alaea to La Perouse Bay, which encompasses Kīhei and Wailea, features more wonderful beaches, while the 10,025-feet Haleakalā towers over East Maui, which includes the lush, green cowboy region known as 'Upcountry'. Hāna, a beautiful, sleepy seacoast area that includes a cattle ranch, holds court at the extreme eastern end of Maui, while the Central Valley features the seat of government at Wailuku and a thriving port and commercial center at Kahului.

RENTALS and TOURS

There are a number of air and land tour companies operating on Maui, most of them very experienced in packaging tours to specific areas. Consult the Yellow Pages of the Maui telephone book for ideas. For exploring on your own, or for sudden, spur-of-the-moment sightseeing or shopping, a rental car is preferable.

There are a variety of ways to get around Maui, but the best is to rent a car. There is a proliferation of car rental agencies on the island, all offering competitive rates.

Public transportation is limited to the **Grayline Maui** (877-5507). It will make pickups at Kahului Airport, but is not a public bus system. It is illegal to hitchhike on Maui. Sample distances in both miles and driving time from Kahului Airport are as follows: Kahului—3 miles, 5 minutes; Wailuku—6 miles, 10 minutes; Kīhei—9 miles, 20 minutes; Lahaina—27 miles, 45 minutes; Kā'anapali—30 miles, 50 minutes; Haleakalā summit—37 miles, one and a half hours; Hāna—52 miles, two and a half hours; Kapalua—36 miles, one hour; Wailea—18 miles, 35 minutes.

Car rentals

More than two dozen rental companies flourish on Maui, and they offer everything from luxury cars to four-wheel drives and subcompacts. Staff at hotel desks can put you in touch with any of them, or you can take advantage of the agencies represented at Kahului and Kapalua-West Maui Airports. Air conditioning is recommended in the summer months of July through September.

Rental agencies caution against driving on the northeast coast, or on the road past Seven Pools near Hāna because the roads are difficult for standard-drive vehicles. A driver's license and major credit card are required.

Nationally known agencies at or near Kahului Airport include: **Avis Rent A Car** (871-7575), **Budget Rent-A-Car Maui** (871-8811), **Dollar Rent A Car** (877-2731), **Hertz Rent A Car** (877- 5167) and **National Car Rental** (871-8851). **Rock-N-Roll Rentals** (874-6936-rents "new" old sportscars), **Word-of-Mouth Rent-A-Car** (877-2436), and **Tropical Rent-A-Car** (877-0002) are also located in Kahului. **Sunshine Rent-A-Car** (661-5646) is located in Lahaina. **Maui Rent A Jeep** (877-6626) offers a discount for senior citizens.

Whatever you select from Maui's wide choices, reserving a car in advance is a good idea; two million visitors a year tend to make rentals scarce at peak visitor times.

DRIVING TIPS

Maui's posted speed limits are realistically set. Major highways generally are good quality, but back country roads tend to be narrow and twisting. Traffic slowdowns from heavy construction or sugarcane and pineapple trucks that crawl down two-lane roads occur often, and motorists must exercise both caution and patience. Most urban centers are relatively easy to drive in, but Lahaina can be traffic-clogged at times, and parking is at a premium. While driving generally is a good experience, there are times to remember the local phrase, 'ain't no beeg t'ing, brah', meaning, 'it's no big deal, take it easy'.

Bicycles and mopeds

It's possible to see Maui on a bicycle if you are both experienced and careful. Long-distance bicycling can be tedious in East Maui, where Haleakalā rises more than 10,000 feet in forty miles. On the other hand, a paved bicycle path from Kā'anapali to Lahaina only three miles away makes bicycling in that area a pleasure. As a result, the bicycle rentals are in West Maui. **A&B Moped Rental** (669-0027), **AA Go Go Bikes Hawaii** (661-3063) offers a variety of bikes and mopeds.

Bicycling tours to the summit of Haleakalā and through the lush region of Upcountry Maui are available. **Cruiser Bob's** (667-7717) takes people to the Haleakalā summit, and lets them coast all the way down. The bikes are equipped with special brakes. The trip includes breakfast going up, lunch coming down, and pickup service in Lahaina. **Maui Downhill** (871-2155) offers a similar package.

Land tours

There are at least two dozen sightseeing tour companies operating on Maui, some of them highly specialized, others prepared to show visitors the best of Maui. For a complete listing see Tours in the Maui Yellow Pages.

Akamai Tours (871-9551) offers air-room-car packages and tours to other islands, and operates minibuses. **Aloha Nui Loa Tours** (669-0000) is based at Kīhei and runs tours to Hāna and up the massive Haleakalā Crater. **Arthur's Rolls**

Cruiser Bob's bike tours wind down Haleakalā Highway.

Royce Limousine Service (661-5466, 800 345-4667) also goes to Hāna and Haleakalā, but in classic limousines. Tom Barefoot's Cashback Tours (661-8889) can arrange all kinds of tours, from sunset sails to off-island adventures. Grayline Maui (877-5507), one of Maui's largest tour operators, provides airport transportation as well as tours. Hana Cassette Guide (572-0550) features informational tapes about Hāna, Haleakalā, and ʻĪao Valley.

Highly specialized tours by the Maui Historical Society (244-3326) are geared toward the visitor with a bent for history. No Ka Oi Scenic Tours (871-9008) covers most of the island in a three-day tour that includes Haleakalā at sunrise and sunset and a buffet lunch in Hāna. Robert's Hawaii (871-6226) also arranges day trips to other islands. Sea Sails (667-7798) operates from the resort area of Kāʻanapali. Trans Hawaiian Maui (877-7308) provides tours and transportation services in vans and stretchouts as well as limousines, and has guides who speak a number of foreign languages. Tours with food service are provided by Tropical Excursions (877-7887) in buses with sun roofs.

Ekahi Tours (572-9775), located in Upcountry Maui, lets visitors see the Hāna area and the lush Keʻanae Peninsula up close.

TAXIS and TROLLEYS

Despite its size, Maui has only a handful of taxi companies, and rides tend to be pricey. In West Maui there are the Alii Cab Co. (661-3688); Inlanda, Inc. (667-7800), offering a senior citizens discount; Kaanapali Taxi (661-5285); Classy Taxi (661-3044); and West Maui Taxi (667-2605). In East Maui, there are Jake's Taxi (877-6139); La Bella Taxi (242-8011); Yellow Cab (877-7000), which services the Kahului Airport; and in Kīhei, Kihei Taxi (879-3000) and Wailea Taxi & Tour (874-5000). The Free Lahaina Express transports passengers from the Kāʻanapali resort area to Lahaina. This closed-in replica of a San Francisco trolley car operates daily from 9am to 5pm.

For departing visitors from the Kāʻanapali area the West Maui Airport Trolley travels daily to the airport during daytime hours, and it is also free.

LIMOUSINES

Maui has two main limousine services, and both operate twenty-four hours a day. Arthur's Rolls Royce Limousine Service (661-5466, 800 345-4667) operates stretch Lincolns all over the island. Chauffeurs wear uniforms and caps, roll out red carpets on occasion, and have been known to fill the car with helium balloons and release them through the sun roof in celebration of weddings or other festive events. Each of Arthur's limousines contains a complimentary bar. Wailea Limousine Services, Inc. (879-8477) and Silver Cloud Limousine Service (669-8580, 800 445-3888) on Maui also have well-deserved reputations for service and style. Chauffeurs are on call around-the-clock.

Silver Cloud operates vehicles

ranging from a Ford van to Cadillacs, Lincolns and a Rolls Royce, one

Air tours

Flights aboard small airplanes and helicopters let visitors see Maui from a wonderfully different perspective. Prices vary depending on the length of flights. Some flights not only include airborne tours of Maui, but also cross over to nearby islands of Lāna'i and/or Moloka'i, or even go on for a day to O'ahu or the island of Hawai'i. Hotel activity desks generally have up-to-date information on rates and routes, or the tour firms themselves can be telephoned directly. Prices

of the few on Maui. The company will plan island tours for you.

islands. **Hawaii Helicopters Inc.** (877-3900) specializes in East Maui tours of Ke'anae, Hāna and Haleakalā and provides video cameras for rent. **Kenai Helicopters** (871-6463) bills itself as Hawai'i's largest helicopter flightseeing service and will show you all of Maui, or leave you on a secluded beach to picnic. **Maui Helicopters** operates from Kahului Airport (877-4333) or from the resort area of Wailea (879-2622), and offers sunset flights. **Pacific Helicopter Tours** (871-9771) will

Pineapple-lined Mānele Road, island of Lāna'i.

change frequently.

Most helicopter services operate out of Kahului Airport. **Alex Air Helicopters** (871-0792) provides aerial tours of West Maui, entire-island flights, and is available for charter and rental service to other

arrange specific tours.

Papillon Helicopters (669-4884), located a mile away from Kapalua-West Maui Airport, has tours ranging from a half-hour to a full day, some with champagne picnics. **Paragon Air** (244-3356) provides air tours that can be coupled with ground tours. **Richard's Helicopters** (871-2882) operates from Kahului Airport and will tailor tours for most budgets. **Blue Hawaiian Helicopters** (871-8844) will fly to all parts of Maui, and to other islands. **Sunshine Helicopters** (871-0722) features both tours and charter services. **Temptation Tours** (878-2911 or 877-8888) offers a helicopter ride one way to or from Hana, and a van sightseeing tour on the opposite leg of the trip. Each tour is limited to six people, and includes a gourmet picnic lunch served at one of Hana's beautiful black sand beaches.

Water tours

Some fine sailing and fishing expeditions in Maui waters can be arranged for those who love to reel in a tasty fish, or enjoy the pull of the sails. For details on fishing charters, sailing hires and other water sports, see SPORTS.

EXTENDED CRUISES

American Hawaii Cruises (550 Kearny Street, San Francisco, CA 94108, 800 227-3666) runs seven-day cruises around the Hawaiian island chain aboard their two historic, thirty thousand-ton sister ships, SS *Constitution* and SS *Independence*, built in 1951. The *Constitution* was re-christened in 1982 by Her Royal Highness Princess Grace of Monaco, who sailed aboard the ship in 1956 with her wedding party. The two ships were refurbished in 1980 and have been serving Hawai'i ever since. They occasionally make trans-Pacific voyages between Honolulu and Seattle, Los Angeles or San Francisco, but are usually found cruising warm Hawaiian waters.

Originating in Honolulu, the ships make similar rounds visiting the islands of Hawai'i, Kaua'i and Maui, with ports of call at Hilo and Kona, Nāwiliwili, and Kahului, where they cross paths. Shipboard accommodations—cabins, staterooms and suites—range in size, location and price and determine the overall cruise fare.

EXPLORING

Sightseeing
Lahaina/Kāʻanapali
Kīhei/Wailea
Beaches

The lower pools of 'Ohe'o Gulch spill into the sea.

SIGHTSEEING

Visitors to Maui could hurry around this lovely island in a day or two, but that would be a waste. There is simply too much to see to rush. Like the other islands, Maui enjoys not only great scenic beauty, but a colorful history. Sights you will want to see often combine beauty and nostalgia, evoking a more gracious time even as you admire their beauty today. You must plan your visit well to enjoy all of these facets of Maui.

Maui residents advise that the best way to see the island is to divide your time among the distinct parts of the island. For example, it's possible in a day-long tour to see the summit of Haleakalā and at the same time visit the Upcountry cowboy town of Makawao, or drive leisurely through the lush greenery of Kula on to sprawling 'Ulupalakua Ranch. Most of the Kapalua area can be seen in a day, while allowing for a leisurely lunch and perhaps some beach time. This requires planning, and to that end we have divided this section into sightseeing districts comparable to the distinctive regions of Maui: Lahaina/Kā'anapali, Kapalua, Kīhei/Wailea, Hāna, Upcountry Maui and Wailuku-Kahului.

LAHAINA/KĀ'ANAPALI

Twenty-three miles from Kahului Airport, or a short six miles from the commuter airport of Kapalua-West Maui, the area of Lahaina and Kā'anapali thrives as a resort region that has heavy overtones of its colorful past. In many ways, this is Maui's heart. The great Kamehameha made this area his seat of government after the conquest of Maui in a famous battle near 'Iao Needle, on the other side of the mountains. The missionaries settled here in the mid-1800s, launching their efforts to convert the Hawaiians to Christianity. It also was the magnet for whaling ships, with as many as 400 ships anchoring off Lahaina. Kamehameha III was a resident of the area when he proclaimed new laws and Hawai'i's first official constitution. A great Hawaiian intellectual, David Malo, studied and worked in Lahaina, and is buried in the hills behind the town.

Lahaina's magnificent views of other islands, its beaches, and its fine climate (although the name in Hawaiian means 'merciless sun') have long attracted visitors. Today, tourism is the lifeblood of the region.

Approaching Lahaina on Highway 30 from Kahului is a fine way to get into the mood of the area; the drive goes around a lava coastline and affords views of the islands of Kaho'olawe and Lāna'i, the islet of Molokini, and, in the distance, the island of Moloka'i. There are several scenic points; during the whale-watching season from December to July, these areas often are crowded with cars.

Here also are small, roadside parks with good ocean views— **Pāpalaua, Ukumehame, Launiupoko** and **Puamana**. They offer a chance to stop, stretch, feel the sun, and enjoy the view. The road winds past **Olowalu**, a community of a few homes, a general store and a good French restaurant, Chez Paul. It is the site of a famous massacre: In a trading dispute the captain of the *Eleanora* turned his ship's guns on Hawaiians in canoes alongside his ship. More than a hundred Hawaiians died in the cannonade, and more than 200 were wounded, many to die in the next few days. That was in 1790, but the massacre is remembered still. Among other consequences, the massacre led to the capture of Isaac Davis and John Young and their ultimate designation as advisors to the ambitious Kamehameha. Young was to become a close friend and was with Kamehameha when the monarch died.

From Olowalu to Lahaina the road continues to curve between the sea and sugarcane fields, and finally leads into the town itself. Some long-time residents look on Lahaina as a classic example of survival: the town has gone from fishing village, to whaling capital of the Pacific, to supplier of goods and staples to the sugar plantations, and finally to the hub of visitor activities on Maui. Some of the old flavor remains in Lahaina—the narrow streets, the buildings hunched against each other, the smell of the sea and the view across the harbor to other islands. The number of visitors walking the streets today at least rivals the crowds of a century ago when Hawaiians, whalers, missionaries and beachcombers all gathered at Lahaina.

Lahaina itself is a National Historic Landmark, and also is protected as a Maui County Historic District. The **Lahaina Restoration Foundation** (661-3262) works hard at seeing interesting old buildings and landmarks refurbished and restored. In 1980 the old seawall, where residents and visitors gathered to watch sunsets, was rebuilt. The **Wo Hing Temple**, built in 1912, has been renovated, and the historic Pioneer Inn has undergone extensive refurbishing. Most of the two-mile stretch of Front Street, the focal point of Lahaina,

Ancient petroglyphs, near Olowalu.

retains its old look and feel despite the modern veneer. For those who want to see Lahaina in a leisurely manner, walk down this street and a few streets beyond, to see the town both as it is and was. Here are some of the major attractions:

In the heart of the town is a ninety-three-foot replica of a nineteenth century brig, *The Carthaginian*; inside is a well-designed, interesting exhibit of whales and whaling. *The Carthaginian* is moored at the dock at the end of Papelekane Street and is open from 9:30am to 4:30pm. There is a small admission charge.

Immediately behind *The Carthag-* a site where early Hawaiians practiced medical arts, is north of *The Carthaginian*.

Near the Hauola Stone is the **Brick Palace**, ordered built by Kamehameha the Great as a residence. It is believed to be the first Western-style building constructed in Hawai'i.

Walk south from *The Carthaginian* down Wharf Street to get to the **Old Lahaina Courthouse**, built in 1859 from the stones of a previous courthouse destroyed by a gale the year before.

Next to the Courthouse is the site of the **Old Fort**, built in the 1830s and used mostly as a prison. The

The bright green and white-trimmed Pioneer Inn, Lahaina's longtime landmark.

inian is the **Pioneer Inn**, built in 1901. It served as West Maui's major hotel until the 1950s. It was renovated in 1964, and is undergoing a second refurbishing. Breakfast on the *lānai* was a favorite of the *kama'āina* [long-time resident] for several generations.

The **Hauola Stone**, believed to be reconstructed fort replaced the one downtown in the late 1850s; its coral block helped make the new prison.

At the end of Wharf Street is a site remembered, not especially fondly, as the place where the government managed a market where Hawaiians traded with whalingmen. The site was known as **Rotten Row.**

On Front Street between Dickenson Street and Papelekane Street are three important historical sites. The **Masters' Reading Room** was built in 1834 by missionaries and ships' officers. Made from blocks of coral, the building is one of the oldest Western structures on Maui, and today is headquarters of the Lahaina Restoration Foundation. The **oldest coral stone house** in the islands is nearby; it was the **home of William Richards**, the first protestant missionary to Lahaina. These two structures flank the **Baldwin Home Museum.**

The Reverend Dwight Baldwin, his wife Charlotte and their eight children lived in the Baldwin Home from 1836 to 1868. The New England-style house contains some of the original furnishings. The home, open daily from 9:30am to 5pm, can be entered for a small admission fee.

Across the street and down by Hotel Street is one of Lahaina's more visible landmarks, a **Banyan Tree** that was planted in 1873 to commemorate the fiftieth anniversary of the arrival of Lahaina's missionaries. Today the tree covers a square—more than half an acre—and is so big its various trunks are propped up in places. It is a convenient meeting place for people, and a bandstand for mynah birds that gather in the early evening to serenade anyone who will listen.

At the corner of Front and Shaw Streets is **Malu'uluoLele Park**, a site which seems unremarkable today but once was a significant part of Lahaina. It contained a pond and a small island where Maui chiefs lived and died. Once it held a mausoleum, but the remains were moved and the pond filled in. Leveling the ground obliterated the physical evidence of its history, but

Sitting on the dock of Lahaina Harbor, watching the boats go by.

old-timers today remember tales from their childhood about spirits lingering in the area.

The first stone church built in the islands—about 1830—is located on Waine'e Street. It was destroyed several times, and its name changed from Waine'e Church to **Waiola Church** [water of life]; Nearby is the **Waine'e Cemetery**, filled with gravestones from the nineteenth century; it is the burial site of Keōpūolani, a queen of Kamehameha the Great.

Also on Waine'e Street, which intersects with Shaw Street, is the **Hongwanji Mission**, a Buddhist meeting place since 1910. The original small building was replaced in 1927 with the present building, which continues to be an important site for West Maui's Buddhists.

A few steps down Waine'e Street from the Buddhist mission is the **homesite of David Malo**, the Hawaiian intellectual who embraced many of the new *haole* teachings, and then feared they would diminish the importance of ancient Hawaiian ways and fought against them.

On the opposite corner is **Hale Pa'ahao**, the old prison, made of the blocks from the Old Fort on Front Street. Built in the 1850s primarily to get rampaging sailors off the street, the prison held inmates whose offenses ranged from murder to riding a horse on Sundays.

Another Buddhist structure, the **Shingon Temple**, is located north on Luakini Street, which is parallel to Waine'e Street. It was built by and for the Japanese laborers who came to Maui near the turn of the century to work in plantation fields.

Luakini Street is significant also because it was the route of the tragic Princess Nāhi'ena'ena's funeral procession. She died at twenty-one, a victim of the conflicts in 1837 that

The imposing two-ton Buddha seems to dwarf the mountains beyond.

pitted the old Hawaiian ways against the new thought brought by the missionaries.

Nāhi'ena'ena had been in love with her brother since they were children together in Lahaina; but now her brother was King Kamehameha III, and the focus of divergent opinions on Hawai'i and its future. Hawaiian tradition would allow Nāhi'ena'ena to marry her brother and bear royal children. To the Hawaiians this was the natural and logical way of perpetuating a dynasty and ensuring stability throughout the land. To the new *haole* missionaries, it was anathema. The king was torn between these viewpoints; Nāhi'ena'ena was shattered, and

Kamehameha III became the classic tale of cultures in conflict, and all people of Hawai'i—whatever their beliefs—mourned. The princess' first funeral was in Honolulu, where the king led a procession of great chiefs behind a simple cart draped in black silk; at the church the service was conducted by one of the most famous missionaries, Hiram Bingham. Kamehameha III then fitted out a ship and sent his sister's body home to Lahaina, where a roadway was cut through groves of breadfruit and *kou*. The cortege with its black-draped coffin moved along a road layered with sand, grass and mats. The lament of the common people could be heard along the route. Nāhi'ena'ena was

'Anaka' leads the Sugarcane Train through Lahaina and Kā'anapali.

became dissolute and wretched. Before her twenty-second birthday the young princess died. Long after her death, the king could be found sitting quietly at her graveside.

The story of Nāhi'ena'ena and

entombed in a mausoleum and remembered forever by her people. Today that route is Luakini Street.

That road ends at Lahainaluna Street, a major entryway into the town itself and along which

Kā'anapali's four-mile beach is still the most popular attraction of the Resort.

Lahainaluna High School and Hale Pa'i are located across the highway and 1.5 miles up in the hills. To reach them you pass the still-functioning **Pioneer Mill**, built in 1860. **Lahainaluna High School** is the oldest school west of the Rockies, opened in 1831 by mission-

aries. In its heyday, the school accepted pupils from other parts of Hawai'i as well as California. An adjunct of the school was **Hale Pa'i Printing House**. It, too, is historic—it published Hawai'i's first newspaper and made Lahaina famous. Hale Pa'i was restored in 1982, and features an exhibit of the early printing press. It is open from 9am to 4pm Monday through Saturday, and charges a small admission fee. If you have paid the admission to the Baldwin Home, admission to Hale Pa'i is included.

Visitors to Hale Pa'i who also want to look around the school are asked to sign in at the vice principal's office. Visitors who are aware of David Malo's contribution to Hawai'i sometimes ask to see his gravesite; he is buried on **Mt Ball**, above the school and near the giant 'L' visible from Lahaina. Back in town and past Lahainaluna Street, visitors still exploring Front Street will come across the **Lahaina Jodo Mission** near Māla Wharf. The Mission contains a Japanese cultural park, with pagodas, temples and a bell tower. This site commemorates the first Japanese immigrants, and in 1968 the centennial of their arrival was celebrated with the dedication of the largest Buddha outside of Asia. The buildings are closed to the public, but visitors may stroll around outside and enjoy the air of serenity. Three miles outside Lahaina on Route 30 is the resort area of Kā'anapali, reachable by car, bicycle (there is a bicycle lane) or on foot. One way of getting there is on the **Lahaina-Kaanapali & Pacific Railroad**; old-timers remark, "the name is longer than the train."

Also called the 'Sugarcane Train', it is a colorful string of three passenger cars pulled by the steam engine 'Anaka' and backed up by a second engine 'Myrtle', both rebuilt to turn-of-the-century specifications. The train chugs between Lahaina and Kā'anapali across a 400-foot-long trestle and beside a championship golf course. They are the most beautiful miles any train could cover, and as an added fillip to the trip, the conductor frequently bursts into song.

Stations at either end of the track are built in Victorian style, as befitting the Hawaiian monarchy era theme. Passenger cars are fitted with wooden seats; the locomotive's cab is trimmed in mahogany. There are five daily departures from the stations, starting at 9:35am and ending at 4:10pm. Tickets may be purchased at hotels or at tour-activities desks, or at the train stations themselves, where jitneys take passengers to and from pickup points in Lahaina and Kā'anapali. Schedules and charges may vary from time to time, so it is best to telephone (661-0089).

Kā'anapali itself is something of a miracle—an incredibly lush and comfortable resort area carved from lava, farmland and scrub brush by one of Hawai'i's oldest companies, Amfac. A string of world-class hotels provides luxurious rooms and suites, while surrounding them are tennis courts, golf courses and a long stretch of dazzling beach. In the center of the hotel complexes is **Whalers Village**, an eight-acre site containing art galleries, whaling artifacts, restaurants and shops. The **Whalers Village Museum** (661-5992), on the third floor of Building G, has what has been called the largest collection of whaling memorabilia in the world, including a thirty-six foot skeleton of a sperm whale. Admission is free.

The **Kaanapali Trolley**, a free jitney service that lets visitors explore this developed site of more than 600 acres, connects the various hotels.

An interesting part of Kā'anapali is **Black Rock** [Pu'u Keka'a], a volcanic formation, eroded by the sea, that was considered a holy place by early Hawaiians. They thought it was one of the places where spirits of the dead left the earth for the spirit world. It also was the place where Maui's most famous king, Kahekili, liked to climb and then leap into the sea. Today the Black Rock has been integrated into the design of the Sheraton-Maui. It is also a good spot for snorkeling; the reef fish are accustomed to visitors.

The wooden sailor at the Pioneer Inn is almost as famous as the hotel itself.

KAPALUA

Highway 30 passes Kā'anapali and heads up to Maui's northwest coast, leading to the resort area of Kapalua and the Nāpili Bay region, an old favorite of many Maui residents.

There is a cutoff from the main highway down to a secondary road, once the principal highway, that leads past restaurants, condominiums and private homes. *Makai* [seaward] of the highway the shoreline alternates between rocks worn smooth by the tides and small, sandy beaches. Just to the north is Kapalua, 750 acres of landscaping, golf courses, tennis courts and

and deep valleys.

Beyond Kapalua, a winding road goes up and down the cliffside past deeply carved bays and Nākālele Point. At one point, at Honokōhau, there are taro fields. On down the road is a large, famous boulder known as the **Bellstone**. When someone strikes one side of the rock, and you listen on the other side, a clear, bell-like sound rings out. Don't be too surprised, though, if you don't hear it. Not everyone does.

The road continues to Kahakuloa, a small, remote town where the villagers like to keep to

Honokōhau Bay.

pools, part of a massive resort complex with the Kapalua Bay Hotel as its focal point.

Kapalua also is famous for its beaches, favorites of local residents who sometimes drive from as far away as Upcountry just to bask in the sun. The area also offers a visual bonus: just across a stretch of blue water, the green island of Moloka'i rises from the sea, giving beach goers a good look at the coves

themselves. Most houses are unpretentious wooden homes. There are two churches, Protestant and Catholic.

Kahakuloa is the most isolated village on Maui, and the road to it from the Central Valley side is rugged. Car rental companies frown on visitors taking rental cars on that stretch of road, but it is possible with a four-wheel-drive vehicle.

Dramatic cliffs near Maui's northernmost tip.

An aerial perspective of sunlit Wailea Beach.

KĪHEI/WAILEA

Maui's southern coast is dry and sunny—a magnet for young beach goers. It also attracted a number of developers over the years who looked at the area's beaches and climate, and forecast a need for housing. The result is a string of condominiums leading from near Mā'alaea, a major boat harbor, on through the Kīhei sector and into Wailea, a glossy resort area with a number of fine hotels. Beyond Wailea lies Mākena, a network of excellent beaches off the beaten path.

To get to Mā'alaea from Kahului Airport, travel on Highway 380 across the isthmus to Highway 30; proceed on 30 until the road veers left into Mā'alaea. You will be at the site of a small boat harbor where the Coast Guard keeps a cutter and where there are a number of charter boats. Waterfront condominiums also are here.

Back on Highway 30 to Highway 31, a well-marked secondary road leads into Kīhei, an area with a growing number of good restaurants and long rows of condominiums. Here too are beach parks— **Maipoina'oeia'u**, at the upper end of Kīhei, and **Kalama** and **Kama'ole Beach Parks** in the heart of Kīhei. Many visitors claim this area has the best combination of beaches, weather and views on Maui, and perhaps in all of Hawai'i. With the addition of new shopping centers and shops, Kīhei is a self-contained spot that caters to a variety of tastes and budgets. From Kīhei's beaches there are excellent views of Haleakalā, the sweep of coastline and the West Maui Mountains off in the distance.

At the other end of Kīhei is a 1450-acre complex of fine hotels, restaurants and shops, with two golf courses, fourteen tennis courts and

Taking an afternoon stroll in Kīhei.

specialty offerings such as scuba diving, snorkeling, hula lessons and windsurfing. This is Wailea, Alexander & Baldwin's jewel-like resort set against the arid lava flows of southeast Maui. The area is still growing; plans have been announced for at least four new hotels. Fortunately, there is ample room at Wailea.

One of the area's great pluses is the string of five excellent beaches, one after the other. Maui's beaches lie like a sandy lei around the island, but here in Wailea they seem to sparkle.

Just down the road is Mākena, undeveloped and unspoiled. It is an area of superb beaches but no amenities. Years ago the area was a semi-permanent campsite for transients, and attained a certain notoriety. One of the beaches, Onouli (residents call it 'Little Mākena') still has a reputation as a nude beach and is subject to occasional police sweeps. Oneloa ('Big Beach' to residents) lies on the other side of the distinctive Pu'uōla'i, a 360-foot cindercone; Big Beach offers not only good swimming but an excellent place to watch the sunset. The Mākena area has no gas stations or water, and is plagued with rough roads; yet, it is beautiful. In the **'Āhihi-Kīna'u Natural Area Reserve**, unusual marine life abounds in the tidal pools and offshore.

South of this natural reserve site is **La Perouse Bay**, marking the spot where, in 1786, the French explorer Comte de La Perouse became the first Westerner to set foot on Maui. La Perouse sailed away from Maui in search of new adventures and disappeared at sea. Today the bay named for this intrepid Frenchman is reachable by four-wheel-drive vehicle. An ancient trail leads from La Perouse Bay on south along the rugged coastline.

Learning how to body board in the smooth surf at Kā'anapali.

HANA

To approach Hāna is to turn back the calendar; it is a place lost in time, existing in one century while wearing the face of another. Even in Maui, itself a special place, Hāna stands apart.

Part of its charm lies in its isolation. There is an airstrip served by a commuter airline, but no facilities that encourage easy air traffic. Most people take the Hāna Highway. Carved from the hillside in 1927, and generally following an old trail; the highway has by some count more than 600 curves, plus fifty-four bridges, and driving it is an experience. (In Hāna, you can buy a T-shirt that boasts, 'I survived the Hana Highway'.)

Just the effort in getting to Hāna makes it a special place. The drive can take about two and a half to three hours from Kahului, depending on how often you stop to look at waterfalls. You will miss a lot if you do not make any stops.

On Highway 36 is **H.A. Baldwin Park**, a good place for camping, swimming and surfing. Just beyond is Pā'ia, Maui's most important town at the peak of the sugar era, and now important to windsurfers because it's near famous Ho'okipa Beach, the mecca of windsurfers from all over the world. Pā'ia's old-town flavor is a mixture of history, the surfing mystique and a laid-back lifestyle.

In the heart of Pā'ia is the **Mantokuji Buddhist Temple**. Down the road is **Twin Falls**, a swimming hole formed by two mountain streams. It is reachable by following a sign posted just under two miles beyond Kākipi Gulch.

Past Twin Falls is the village of **Huelo**, and shortly after that a second small town, **Kailua**. These are the quiet, sleepy places that add

51

Just before the paved road ends in Kīpahulu, Hāna Coast.

to the aura of peace and contentment along the northeast coast. As the road winds past them, the incredibly lush foliage cloaks the roadside. Drink in, too, the beauty of the streams and waterfalls.

Past Kailua are **Kaumahina State Park** and Honomanū County Park. The former has restrooms, picnic tables and pavilions, and a commanding view of the Keʻanae Peninsula ahead and Honomanū Bay down below. Below, at **Honomanū Park**, there is a lovely, small black sand beach, although the park has no amenities and the swimming can be treacherous. A short distance on down the highway is **Keʻanae Valley Lookout,**

Hawaiian staple from which *poi* is made. Here also are many other types of native Hawaiian plants.

Down on the peninsula modern taro farms look much like their older counterparts. Many of the area's residents are Hawaiians who hold on to the old ways.

The next stop is Wailua, remarkable for its well-known Coral Miracle Church. The church's real name is actually **St Gabriel's Church**. When parishoners set out to build a church in 1870, they found sand and coral washed ashore, which they used as building materials.

Past Wailua is **Nāhiku**, a rain-swept site three miles down from the highway, and once the location of a rubber plantation. At the turn of the century Nāhiku was believed to be the only place in America where rubber was grown commercially. Today there are still a few rubber trees in evidence. Two good swimming holes are

St Gabriel's Church, Hāna.

where you can admire views of Wailua in one direction and Keʻanae Valley and up to Koʻolau Gap in the other.

Before heading down a side road to **Keʻanae Peninsula**, stop at the **Keʻanae Arboretum**. It features reconstructed old taro patches and some sixty varieties of taro, the

located here, one reached from the landing, one via a path on the right after the village's two churches.

The road leads into Hāna from Nāhiku. A turnoff on Alaino Road takes visitors down to a botanical garden with a broad variety of plants, near a massive old *heiau*, on private land. The **Piʻilanihale**

Heiau is said to be the largest in the islands, with huge walls still intact. Only a mile away, at the next turnoff, is Hāna's airstrip.

Just past the airstrip turnoff is a side road that leads to Wai'ānapanapa State Park, a dramatic seacoast area of great natural beauty. Trails lead through the Wai'ānapanapa and Waimao Caves. Like most other Hawaiian areas, Wai'ānapanapa has both legend and fact, and they occasionally meld. Wai'ānapanapa Cave is partially filled with water, which turns red in the spring. Folklore has it that a jealous husband traced his wife, a princess, to the cave and killed her; others blame the color on

beach fringes the small bay, where swimming is good when the water is calm.

From the black sand beach it's possible to follow a trail along the seacoast. The trail was part of the King's Highway, a sixteenth century construction project spearheaded by Chief Pi'ilani. Today it takes about two hours to cover the three miles into Hāna. There is tent camping in Wai'ānapanapa, and cabins that have electricity, bedding, water and a kitchen.

Back on the highway and just outside the town of Hāna is Helani Gardens, a seventy-acre nursery started some thirty years ago and opened to the public in 1975. The

Ancient ruins of a Hawaiian village in the vast Haleakalā National Park.

tiny red shrimp. Some people on Maui who find spiritual power in certain sites claim that Wai'ānapanapa is a place of great spirituality.

Beyond the caves, along the shoreline, a natural blowhole and a high arch distinguish the point. Nearby Honokalani black sand

lower acreage is manicured and trimmed, the upper sixty-five acres left wild for those who like to wander among a variety of strange plants. One section contains a treehouse built mostly by the grandchildren of the founder of the Gardens; the treehouse contains windows, electricity and plumbing.

One of the deep caves at Wai'ānapanapa State Park.

Helani Gardens is open daily, 10am to 4pm (248-8274) and charges a small admission fee.

In Hāna town, the pace is easy and the sights are heart-warming. The town's population is mostly Hawaiian, with a sprinkling of celebrities who have found the town's quiet ways to their liking. The homes and the few shops huddle in the arm of **Ka'uiki Head**, a volcanic outcropping. Rising above the town on a *pu'u* [hill] is a large cross, memorial to Paul Fagan, who founded the Hāna Ranch and the area's landmark, the **Hotel Hana-Maui**. From the cross there is a spectacular view of the town and bay.

Stop and relax in this lovely town. This is the place where, for years when you telephoned the police department, you got a recorded message: "...if this is an emergency, leave your name and number and we'll call you back." This also is the town where Sunday services at **Wānanalua Church** are conducted both in Hawaiian and English.

Hale Waiwai O Hāna, a museum near the turnoff to Hāna Bay, chronicles the colorful and some-times turbulent past of Hāna. This was the birthplace of Ka'ahumanu, who became the favorite (and strong-willed) wife of Kamehameha I, whose armies crushed the Maui armies in a battle that ranged near Ka'uiki Head. Hāna evolved into a plantation town, but sugar began to diminish as an area industry in the 1940s, and many people left Hāna for employment elsewhere. San Francisco industrialist Paul Fagan bought 14,000 acres and converted them into a cattle ranch; he also built the Hotel Hana-Maui.

The Museum is housed in the

Hāna Cultural Center (Uakea Road 248-8622), open 11am to 4pm (times subject to change) Mondays through Saturdays. Visitors are asked to make a small donation. There is a park with public tennis courts near the center of town, and down along the bay an old pier affords a good look back at Hāna. From the pier a trail goes off to the right and onto Ka'uiki Head—not an easy walk—and to a site where a plaque marks Ka'ahumanu's birthplace.

Hasegawa General Store, a long-time Hāna landmark, was burned down in the summer of 1990, but is scheduled for rebuilding soon. A fixture just south of town, the old store brimmed with staples, souvenirs—and visitors. Hasegawa's was celebrated some years ago in a song by Paul Weston's band that was a national hit.

Past Hāna town the sense of isolation continues. The road continues to wind down the coastline, marked by waterfalls and small bridges over cool streams. This is Highway 31 and leads into Kīpahulu, a part of Haleakalā National Park. En route you pass **Hāmoa Beach**, open to the public but with facilities off-limits except to Hotel Hana guests.

Wailua and **Kanahuali'i Falls** are seven miles out of Hāna. A trail leads down to a rocky beach where a settlement was wiped out in April 1946 by a tsunami (a tidal wave generated by an earthquake). Above the road is a concrete cross, honoring one Helio, a Hawaiian Catholic who lived during the 1840s and converted hundreds of people to Catholicism. Not far away is a roadside shrine containing an Italian marble statue, always draped in fresh flower leis.

Now inside the National Park,

visitors always admire 'Ohe'o Gulch, an area where twenty-four pools topple one into another and finally into the sea. This is known, erroneously, as Seven Sacred Pools, or **Seven Pools**. A path on the left bank of the Palikea Stream leads down to fine swimming and picnicking areas. On the other side and some distance above are taro farms maintained by the Cultural Center in Hāna. There are conducted tours of this area by National Park Rangers (248-8251 for information).

A trail takes visitors who want to hike up Waimoku Falls Trail to **Makahiku Falls**, a half mile away, and then two more miles on to **Waimoku Falls** (see Hiking under SPORTS).

At Kīpahulu Ranch the paved road ends. Famed aviator Charles A. Lindbergh is buried a short walk away from the gate on the *makai* side of the road in the churchyard of **Palapala Ho'omau Church**. Lindbergh spent much of his later years in Hāna and helped restore the church. Before his death he picked his burial site.

Most car rental companies ban renters from driving in the area beyond Kīpahulu. It is a gravel road linking Kīpahulu with the small town of **Kaupō**, eight miles away, best reached in a four-wheel-drive vehicle.

Kaupo Store is the heart of the town, and is not only the town's supplier but its post office as well. The town also contains **Kuialoha**

Church, built in 1859 and since restored. On a hill above the road are the remains of a *heiau*; a second larger one lies at the head of the Kaupō Gap Trail behind the small school.

The road from Kaupō to 'Ulupalakua Ranch is difficult, even with four-wheel-drive vehicles, but exciting. Along the way are great views along the coastline. Past the old **Nu'u Landing** and at the end of a dry creekbed, there are caves and petroglyphs (Hawaiian rock carvings). In the distance you will see Molokini Island, and beyond it the island of Kaho'olawe.

At 'Ulupalakua visitors enter the Upcountry area. From the ranch region the road winds back down through Kula and you are suddenly a world away from remote Hāna.

A word of caution: The road past Kīpahulu is difficult and demanding, and should not be attempted without proper clothing, gear, water, emergency equipment, nor without notifying someone of your intentions. You should carry extra gas in jerrycans, depending on your vehicle. In any case, it is a good idea to check with Park Rangers and/or residents of the area before making the long drive around the Hāna Coast, then attempting the sortie to 'Ulupalakua. Additionally, just to get to Hāna town from the West Maui resort area is a full day, a drive one-way of five to six hours. The trip is rewarding, but to attempt more than that requires planning and forethought.

The ever changing and timeless beauty of the Hāna Coast.

EXPLORING/Sightseeing

58

UPCOUNTRY MAUI

For most visitors, Upcountry is a different—and unexpected—world. It reminds many travelers of Wyoming, in that it is cool, green and dotted with cattle ranches. The mood is decidedly Western, with cows, horses, four-wheel-drive vehicles, cowboy hats, rail fences and temperatures much cooler than at Maui's lower elevations.

On the slopes of Haleakalā, pheasant and francolin can be seen against the green grasses. A wide variety of flowers grow here, including the exotic protea, a South African plant that is hardy, varied and colorful, and proving to be a lucrative export for Maui growers.

Protea is sold at roadside stands off Highways 377 and 378. The famous Kula onion grows here as well. Jacaranda trees line some back roads, and from almost everywhere above the 1500-foot level, there are magnificent vistas of the ocean and of West Maui.

Highways 37, 377 and 378 lead to Haleakalā, and wind through Upcountry. Off Highway 37 is Makawao Avenue, leading to the unpretentious cowboy town of Makawao, which somehow contin-ues to change, and yet, in some ways, stays the same. You pass horses as well as cars along the town's main route of Baldwin Avenue. To the right of Highway 37 at the road's only traffic light is a shopping center, the town of Pukalani, and the Pukalani Terrace Golf Course and Country Club.

Highway 37 melds into 370, leading to 'Ulupalakua Ranch and a small visitor center where it is possible to buy wines grown on the ranch. The ranch owner, C. Pardee Erdman, and a young wine-maker from California, Emil Tedeschi, combined their talents to produce Hawai'i's first commer-cial wine. The 2000-foot elevation and the Carnelian grape made the wine produced by Tedeschi Vineyards, Ltd., a commercial and aesthetic success. The ranch road winds to a

Octagonal Church of the Holy Ghost, Upcountry.

tasting room where the wines and other local products are displayed and sold.

The drive to 'Ulupalakua from the Central Valley area should take an hour and a half or so, without rushing. It goes past pristine Kēōkea Park, a good place to picnic. It also goes past a famous octagonal church in Kula, the **Church of the Holy Ghost**. This 1897 Catholic church on the hillside above Waiakoa has a large altar that had to be shipped in sections around Cape Horn.

Not far away off Highway 377 is the **Kula Botanical Gardens**, with more than 700 plants (the protea among them), rest areas and a picnic table. On another site in

37 onto Copp Road, south of Kula Elementary School.

Above Makawao on Highway 39 is the small community of Olinda, largely untouched by time. Downhill from Makawao, Baldwin Avenue leads into the town of Pā'ia, site of a sugar mill and fast becoming known around the world as the headquarters for Maui's burgeoning windsurfing industry. For those with a four-wheel-drive vehicle and an urge to get off the beaten path, there is the 10.5-mile trip on Waipoli Road from Highway 377 to Polipoli Springs State Recreation Area. To call the road 'unimproved' is an understatement; it can be a real chore to get to the end of the road. Once there, you are in the middle of

Upcountry's clouds are as much a part of the scenery as its pastures.

Kula, the **University of Hawai'i College of Tropical Agriculture** operates a twenty-acre **Experimental Station** where important research takes place—and lovely roses grow. The site is off Highway

a hardwood forest. If you climb another thousand feet on foot, you can stand atop a volcanic cinder cone and enjoy an astonishing view of other islands. There is a single cabin in the area that can be re-

Moody skies accompany the ascending Haleakalā Highway.

served through the State Parks office in Wailuku (244-4354).

Dominating the Maui scene is the spectacular **Haleakalā**.

Haleakalā is a volcano 33 miles long and 10,023 feet high. The circumference is 21 miles, the area of the crater 19 square miles. The crater itself is 7.5 miles long, 2.5 miles wide. The national park area surrounding the volcano is 42.6 square miles. One end of the crater gets less than thirty inches of rain a year, while the other end gets more than 300. Hikers and campers in the crater can—and often do—get sunburned and rained on in the western rim of the summit. From there, the road takes visitors on a series of switchback turns in increasingly frigid temperatures to the 10,023-foot summit. There is no public transportation to Haleakalā, and visitors must use rental cars, taxis or tour vehicles to visit the area.

The views are spectacular. The road winds through ranchlands, and with each turn offers a view of the land below, of West Maui's mountains (usually peeking through a cloud cover, particularly in the afternoon). In the distance are islands—inhabited Moloka'i and

The desolate fascination of Haleakalā Crater.

same day. For current weather conditions, call 871-5054.

The most direct way to Haleakalā is to drive on Highway 37 from Kahului, then, just above Pukalani, veer left onto Highway 377. You will come to another left turn, onto Highway 379 for the last few miles to the **Visitor Center of Haleakalā National Park**, on the western rim of the summit.

Lāna'i, the military target island of Kaho'olawe, and the islet of Molokini. Some hundred miles to the south are the tops of the volcanic massifs of Mauna Loa and Mauna Kea on the Big Island of Hawai'i.

Four overlooks permit breathtaking views of the crater itself. They are **Leleiwi**, at the 9000-foot level; **Kalahaku**, two miles below the summit; the **National Park Visitor Center** near the summit; and the **Red Hill Visitor Center**, Pu'u 'Ula'ula, the top of the mountain.

At the summit is a cluster of white, somewhat-futuristic buildings and domes. This is **Science City**, home of a communications station, University of Hawai'i observatories, radar installations, television relay stations and a satellite tracking station. It is from this area that laser beams have been aimed at satellites as part of the Strategic Defensive Initiative, better known as 'Star Wars'. The site is off-limits.

One fourth of a mile above the park entrance, a paved road leads to the **Hosmer Grove Campground** and picnic area, a half mile from the highway. The area contains a shelter against inclement weather, and includes tables and charcoal

pits. Charcoal pits also are in an open site just below the road. There are tent sites, running water and parking. There is no charge for camping here, but permits are necessary from Park Headquarters (572-9306/7749), or by writing PO Box 369, Makawao 96768.

Park Headquarters, at the 7000-foot level and just a mile inside the park entrance, is a good place to start your visit in this area. The headquarters' hours are 7:30am to 4pm. Inside the building is a wealth of information on Haleakalā, including maps, photographs, a slide presentation and friendly Park Rangers who can answer any question about this unique site. Here is where hiking and camping permits are issued.

Those are the facts of Haleakalā; but like the islands themselves, more than facts are necessary for a

Sunset viewers on the summit of Red Hill, Pu'u 'Ula'ula.

real understanding of this incredible mountain. For example, on some late afternoons at Leleiwi Overlook, your shadow is thrown against the clouds, frequently encircled by a rainbow. Local people call it the 'Spectre of the Brocken'. Stop to enjoy the variety of trees along the trail at Hosmer Grove Campground; some are from India, Japan and Australia. Many people make the effort to see a sunrise on Haleakalā—a spectacular sight, when it's clear—but sunsets are just as rewarding. To see the sun drop behind the West Maui Mountains and watch the sky invent new colors is a never-to-be forgotten experience. A thrilling part of the Haleakalā experience is viewing the crater from the summit, watching the sun break over the cinder cones that jut up from the crater floor. To the east the Big Island forms out of

the darkness, then the sun soars well above the horizon, changing the whole spectrum of colors. To view dawn at Haleakalā means enduring a two-and-a-half- to three-hour drive for those staying at West Maui resorts. It is best to call a direct weather recording (572-7749) before starting up, but warm clothing is never out of place at the summit, which can be twenty-five to thirty degrees (F) colder than Maui's lower elevations. In winter months, it is possible to encounter snow; occasionally snow forces the closing of the road for a time.

Inside the crater there is a desert-like atmosphere. There are lichens, pili grass, clover, evening primrose, 'ōhelo, māmane, tarweed, 'ōhi'a and the rare silversword plant (Argyroxiphium sandwicense). The beautiful silversword is a well-known member of the same family

Racing up to Haleakalā Crater before the sun rises.

as sunflowers, asters and chrysan-themums. The plant grows as long as twenty years and gets as high as eight feet, with a hundred to 500 flower heads.

Outside the crater, on the slopes of the volcano, the *nēnē*, nearly extinct at one point, is fighting its way back. Thoughtful visitors

admire these birds but do not disturb them or disrupt their activities. Generally there are tame *nēnē* around Park Headquarters who are accustomed to visitors snapping photos.

Persons with high blood pressure or a heart condition should remember to move slowly in the rarefied air of upper Haleakalā; such persons are advised not to hike or drive alone.

Haleakalā is justly called 'The House of the Sun', but legends vary on how the demigod Māui, for whom the island is named, accomplished the feat that earned the massive volcano its name.

Legend has it that Māui, the son of Hina, slowed the sun in its passage to give his mother more time to dry tapa [bark cloth]; the sun had simply been passing overhead too quickly. Maui accomplished this from his stance on the summit of Haleakalā, but exactly how depends on what legend you want to believe.

One says that Māui fashioned a giant net—he was a fisherman of renown—and caught the sun as it was streaking overhead. Another legend uses the lariat theory: The prankster caught the sun by its legs as, one by one, the sunlight fell in shafts of light into the crater. He then tied the legs to an 'ōhi'a tree and forced a promise from the sun that it would travel much more slowly across the sky, giving Hina—and women everywhere—more time to accomplish their tasks.

Whichever you prefer, even if you accept the scientific version of Haleakalā's formation by a continuing series of mighty eruptions, the result is a stunning landscape that never fails to awe those who see it. To gaze on Haleakalā is to look at one of the true wonders of the world.

Two years ago the National Park Service began charging admission to Hawai'i's national parks; admission is collected at the Park entrance, but

the visit is well worth the price.

Two additional adventures are possible in Haleakalā—hiking or riding horses into the crater. Inside the crater are three cabins which can accommodate parties up to twelve people, and are rented via the Park Service (see ACCOMMODATION).

WAILUKU-KAHULUI

Central Maui was formed by the gradual joining of lava flows from Haleakalā and the West Maui Mountains. This broad isthmus is the site of thousands of acres of sugar cane, which is harvested by first burning it. The sight of dark smoke rising from the fields startles some visitors, but the practice is accepted and widely used. Occasionally the debris of the burning cane, black flakes often referred to as 'Hawaiian snow', drifts over a town or residential area, forcing residents to close their windows until it passes.

Within the area are two of Maui's major towns, and its commercial heart. Kahului, where the airport is located, also is a deep-water port. Three miles toward the mountains is Wailuku. It is the capital of Maui, the seat of government, and still a charming, old-fashioned town with twisting streets and old wooden structures.

Kahului is Maui's supply center—it contains the shops and stores where staples are sold. When Maui residents go 'to town' for gas, groceries, clothing, furniture or building materials—they are talking about Kahului. Much of what they buy is contained in three shopping malls, all in a row along the main street of Ka'ahumanu Avenue, named for a favorite wife of Kamehameha I. As you move toward Wailuku, they are the Maui Mall, Kahului Shopping Center and Kaahumanu Center. All have a variety of shops and restaurants and ample parking. Hours generally are from 9am to 5pm, but some specialty shops stay open later.

There are several places of interest as you head toward Wailuku from the airport. The first is adjacent to the airport itself—**Kanahā Beach Park**, reachable via Alahao Street just off the baseyard road to the Department of Water Supply. The park has restrooms, parking space, large shade trees, and a view across Kahului Harbor. The park generally is uncrowded and overlooked by most visitors. Between the airport and town is Kanahā Pond, a protected wildlife refuge and home of the migratory Hawaiian stilt, or *ae'o* (Himantopus mexicanus). **Kanahā Pond** formerly was a royal fishpond and now is one of the few places in Hawai'i where the stilt can breed and feed unmolested.

The harbor near the edge of town has become important to Maui as a place where goods are received, and to the Japanese fishermen as a fueling base for their boats. Cruise ships also dock here. Here also is the State's first bulk sugar plant. Next to the harbor is a small park, **Hoaloha Park**, a good place to picnic off the beaten path.

Take the Waiehu Beach Road in the center of town to **Haleki'i**, a partially restored *heiau*, or Hawaiian temple, just outside of Kahului. It can be reached by turning off Waiehu Beach Road onto Kūhiō Place, which is just past a bridge over Īao Stream. Haleki'i was in use during the reign of Maui's famous King Kahekili in the late 1700s. An on-site diagram explains the layout of the walls and terraces. A path leads from the site toward the mountains, and ends in a second temple about a hundred yards away. The second site, **Pihana**, dates from 1779 and was a sacrificial temple. From the Haleki'i site there is an especially good panoramic view of Kahului Harbor.

Wailuku is an easy place to sightsee on foot. The same Ka'ahumanu Avenue that runs through the center of Kahului melds directly into Wailuku's Main Street. That goes on to become 'Iao Valley Road and leads directly into 'Iao Valley. If you park near the town's only 'high rise', the nine-story **Kalana O Maui** (County Office Building), you can see most things of interest just by strolling around.

Across High Street from the County Office Building area is the **Wailuku Library**, which is home to a fine Hawaiiana collection. Just a few steps down from the library is **Ka'ahumanu Church**, built in 1876 and now a Wailuku landmark. The church was the third built by Maui's first Christian congregation. It replaced an earlier building dating from 1832, which had replaced the grass-thatched original where Queen Ka'ahumanu used to attend services.

An interesting way to sample the flavor of Maui is to attend the church service at 9am Sundays. While the service is in English, the invocation and the hymns are in Hawaiian. These powerful voices not only sing praises—they link the present with the past. The church itself is closed during the week, but visitors generally can find the caretaker by walking around to the back of the church. Justly proud of the church, the caretaker usually gives visitors a good-natured, off-hours tour.

If you continue down High Street, which becomes Highway 30, for three miles, you will come to the town of Waikapū. This is the site of the **Maui Tropical Plantation**, sixty

Swards of green sugar cane border Mokulele Highway in the Central Valley.

acres of beautifully kept agricultural park. Open 9am to 5pm with free admission, the park shows Hawaiian plants and fruits in a pleasant landscaped environment. A tram ride, for a fee, winds through the fields of coffee, guava, mango and many other tropical plants. There is a market where many of these products may be purchased.

At the intersection of High Street and Main Street, the road winds on into ʻIao Valley, a three-mile drive alongside ʻIao Stream. Just off to the left as you leave High Street is the **Bailey House Museum**, consisting of two buildings: the home built by Edward Bailey in 1841 when he was head of the Wailuku Female Seminary, and the kitchen-dining room of the school, built in 1838. Also known as the Old Bailey House, the home is made of twenty-inch-thick stone walls covered with plaster and goat hair, and sandalwood beams carved by hand.

Bailey was principal of the school until 1849, when the school closed and he was forced into other employment. As a painter he left a perception of his times that are valuable today. His paintings hang in the Museum. The complex is the **Maui Historical Society Museum**, which houses important traditional Hawaiian artifacts, from tapa cloth to tools to furniture. In back of the building is a canoe shed and other exhibits. The Bailey House Museum is open 9am to 3:30pm daily. There is an admission charge, and conducted tours can be arranged (244-3326).

Two miles along the same road from Wailuku is a Maui County park known as **Kepaniwai Heritage Gardens**, where there are picnic tables with the ʻIao Stream flowing nearby. There is a formal garden with structures representing the peoples of Hawaiʻi, such as the Portuguese outdoor oven, the Chinese moon gate, the Japanese tea house and the Hawaiian grass-woven house. There is no admission charge. The Gardens also provide excellent backdrops for photographs, or just a comfortable place for a respite from sightseeing.

The area was not so comfortable for Maui warriors in 1790, when the forces of Kamehameha I clashed in a bloody battle with the men from Maui. Seemingly invincible, Kamehameha's army defeated the Mauians in a battle that gave the place its name, Kepaniwai— 'damming of the waters', indicating that the Wailuku Stream was

Tombstone by the sea, Mantokuji Buddhist Temple.

blocked by the bodies of the defeated Maui fighters. Today, however, the area is a place of gentleness and peace.

At the end of the road is 'Iao **Valley State Park**. 'Iao is a multifaceted Hawaiian word bound up in the concept of light and supremacy. The park contains its own grandeur. Soaring green mountains and strands of clouds give the park a certain majesty. Near the center of it all is 2250-foot 'Iao **Needle**, a sharprising and heavily eroded peak that forms a dramatic centerpiece for the park. Trails lead up to the top of a ridge for a closer view of the Needle, and down to the stream through a variety of exotic foliage. It is easy to see why Mark Twain called this area, "The Yosemite of the Pacific."

Look for another attraction in the valley. Before reaching the park area, in a part of the valley known as **Pali 'Ele'ele** [dark gorge], there is a sweeping curve where visitors often stand and gaze at boulders on a distant ridge. The boulders are said to form a likeness of the late President John F. Kennedy. This phenomenon, like beauty, is in the eye of the beholder. Some people see the resemblance; others do not.

Wailua Falls, Hāna.

BEACHES

A lei of sandy beaches encircles Maui, as good or better than any in Hawai'i, and among the best in the world. Maui's splendid shores delight the eye—waves curling up on the curving sand, or smooth rocks smashed and rolled by breaking waves whose booming sound is heard far inland. The beaches beckon residents and visitors alike to the old, restless ocean. They also hold tales of Maui's past. The great Kamehameha I's war canoes rendezvoused at the beaches before sailing onward in waves of conquest that brought all the islands under his control. The first European to set foot on Hawai'i did so on a Maui beach (La Perouse in 1786). As a rule, the tides off Maui do not fluctuate as sharply as they do off some of the other islands, but the sea still must be approached with respect and caution. Only then will visitors derive safety and pleasure from the eighty or so beaches that fringe Maui.

WARNINGS

Lifeguards are a rare sight on Maui beaches, and residents and visitors alike must exercise common sense on a beach outing. Heed all warning signs posted at beaches. Some other hazards are listed here, not to discourage ocean enthusiasts but to diminish the dangers and enhance your holiday fun.

Be careful not to spoil your visit by spending too much time in the sun during your first day or two. The sun in Hawai'i is much harsher than in more northerly (or quite southerly) climates. This calls for sunscreen for all but the most acclimatized and dark-skinned individuals. Use sunscreen and limit your time in the sun to an hour or so the first day—depending on the fairness of your skin. You can increase this by ten or twenty minutes a day as you gradually develop a tan.

One of the gravest potential dangers of the deep is the caprice of waves. People who know the sea can observe the cycles of the waves and judge fairly accurately what the surface action will be. There are,

however, freak waves that surprise even the experts. 'Typical' wave action varies with the local shoreline and the season. Call 871-5054 for recorded information on current surf conditions around the island.

Places where waves break directly on or near the shore with dramatic downward force are known as shorebreaks and can be very dangerous for swimmers and bodysurfers. Neck and back injuries can be sustained by turning your back on or trying to jump over or through a large incoming wave. The trick is to take a deep breath and dive *under* the wave.

Another potential danger at such beaches is the backwash, water which has been washed onto the shore and must run back again to the sea. On steep beaches, or after the arrival of particularly voluminous waves, the force of this water can be almost as powerful as the incoming wave and can sweep a person off his or her feet and out to deeper water.

This water rushing back to the sea sometimes gets trapped by other incoming waves and can build to a considerable volume. When this happens, the only way it can move is sideward, creating a rip current that runs along the beach until it finds a deeper bottom. If you find yourself caught in a rip, the best course of action is to flow along with it until its force diminishes. Don't exhaust yourself trying to swim against it. It's easier and safer to walk back along the beach to the place where you started than to fight the water. Some rip currents flow straight out to sea through channels in the reef. If you are caught in one of these, swim to the side of it to get out. This type of rip is far more dangerous.

Sometimes this backed-up water cannot find an outlet and must flow back out *under* the incoming wave. This creates the condition known as undertow. An undertow is a brief phenomenon, lasting only until the wave has passed. For a person pulled down in an undertow, a few seconds under water can seem much longer. Remain calm and come up for air on the other side of the wave.

Another potentially dangerous wave action is the collision of deep ocean swells with rock ledges. It is never safe to venture out to the edge of rocks where surf is breaking. Freak waves can wash over the rocks without warning and many unsuspecting people have been swept away by such waves.

Underwater ledges, too, can present some danger from the surprise of a sudden dropping away of the bottom. Very shallow water can become very deep without notice, so non-swimmers should always keep away from such areas.

Staying safe inshore on a windy day.

EXPLORING/Beaches

72

RATINGS

We have rated Maui's beaches according to our interpretation of certain criteria. We have given the highest priority to safety, access, the presence of facilities (restrooms, showers, picnic tables, barbecue pits, parking), and the composition of the beach itself. Not everyone will agree with the ratings because people look for different qualities when searching for the beach they want to frequent. Maui is blessed with a variety of beaches. Some, such as Nāpili, Fleming's or Oneloa, afford great views. Others, such as the beaches at Mākena, are far enough off the beaten track to remain relatively uncrowded. Hāmoa Beach, at Hāna, is a little jewel-like beach that is every person's dream of a tropical paradise, while the stretch of sand at Kā'anapali is long, wide and unblemished.

Our rating indicators are as follows:

Pure paradise	★★★★★
Superb	★★★★
Excellent	★★★
Good	★★
Fair	★

Additionally, we have indicated by colors beaches that have acceptable conditions for body surfing ● (includes body boarding), board surfing ●, windsurfing ●, snorkeling ● and swimming ●. Scuba diving areas are listed in SPORTS, since a beach is not needed to scuba dive .

Our listing begins with the beaches in West Maui and moves in a counterclockwise direction around the island.

Patterns of early risers' footprints, Kā'anapali Beach.

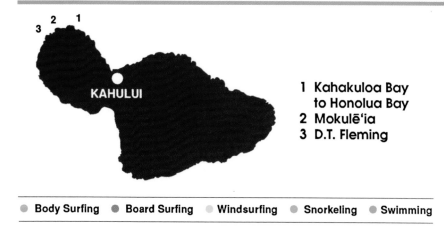

1 Kahakuloa Bay
to Honolua Bay
2 Mokulē'ia
3 D.T. Fleming

● Body Surfing ● Board Surfing ● Windsurfing ● Snorkeling ● Swimming

LAHAINA/KĀ'ANAPALI

1 Kahakuloa Bay to Honolua Bay ★★★★ (scenic/historic significance)

The lovely shoreline along this northwest end of Maui holds an important spot in the hearts of Hawaiians. This is where the Polynesian voyaging canoe *Hōkūle'a* left for its epic journey across the Pacific. Drive along the coastline, and admire the dramatic sea cliffs. Water enthusiasts, however, would be wise to go elsewhere. The ocean is difficult to reach and certainly too hazardous to go in to unless you are a strong swimmer. Maui surfers go to several spots along this coast to perfect their skills, but visitors likely would be happier at the more popular areas with easier access and fewer hazards.

On May 1, 1976, the Polynesian voyaging canoe *Hōkūle'a*, a replica of an old Polynesian sea-going, double-hulled canoe, left from Honolua Bay to sail in the wake of the ancient voyagers. The purpose was to prove that Polynesian voyages of discovery were deliberate, not accidental; that Polynesian navigation, without instruments or clocks could still be accomplished; and that Polynesian pride was well-earned in ocean journeys that eclipsed anything being achieved in the Europe of that time. A month after it sailed, the *Hōkūle'a* reached the island of Mataiwa, 168 miles north of Tahiti, then sailed on into Papeete to a tumultuous welcome.

2 Mokulē'ia ★ ●●●

The summer waves attract bodysurfers to this scenic beach park, but ocean conditions make it too hazardous for other water sports. No fishing is allowed offshore because this is a Marine Life Conservation District. Residents call this beach 'Slaughterhouse' after Honolulu Ranch built a slaughterhouse on the site. It was torn down in the late 1960s.

3 D.T. Fleming Beach Park ★★★★ ●●●●

Most water sports are possible at this scenic beach, but caution is advised. The beach can be hazardous in some conditions, and an eye should be kept on

EXPLORING/Beaches

LAHAINA/KĀ'ANAPALI

the incoming swells. There is some confusion about the name of this beach park—some people think it refers to the beach at Kapalua, sometimes known as Fleming's Beach. The park honors community leader D.T. Fleming (1881-1955), who was born in Scotland but adopted Maui, and was involved in many facets of community life here. The park includes restrooms, paved parking and public access.

4 Kapalua ★★★★ ●●●

Perhaps the most stunningly beautiful of all Maui beaches, Kapalua has been a Maui favorite for years. It was known as Fleming's Beach (after David T. Fleming, area resident and businessman). This is a curving, white sand beach sheltered by two rocky lava arms with clear, calm waters ideal for snorkeling and an excellent view of Moloka'i. Access to the beach is at the south end. There is a paved parking lot and restrooms.

74

5 Nāpili Bay ★★★★ ●●●●

A long, curving beach rims this beautiful bay that is sheltered by rocky outcroppings. This picturesque beach affords a splendid view of Moloka'i, which

Taking the kids for a swim in Kīhei's calm surf.

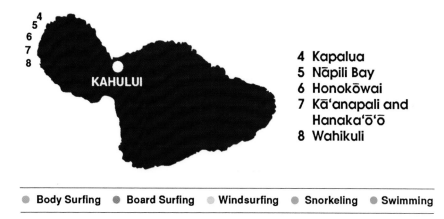

4 Kapalua
5 Nāpili Bay
6 Honokōwai
7 Kāʻanapali and
   Hanakaʻōʻō
8 Wahikuli

KAHULUI

● Body Surfing   ● Board Surfing   ● Windsurfing   ● Snorkeling   ● Swimming

looms large and seemingly close. Winter months can bring larger surf and good conditions for board surfing, and generally the swimming is excellent. There are several public rights of way to the beach.

6 Honokōwai Beach Park ★★★ ●●

This narrow white sand beach features a good spot for children to play in the water. Past the rocks on the beach lies a good area for snorkeling, but only fair for swimming. The park includes a paved parking area, restrooms, picnic tables and showers.

7 Kāʻanapali and Hanakaʻōʻō ★★★★★ ●●●●●

The wide, clean, curving beaches of Kāʻanapali are among the most photo-graphed in the world. Nearby, Hanakaʻōʻō, called 'Sand Box Beach' by residents, is narrow at the south end but broadens as it rounds to the attractive area around Hanakaʻōʻō Point. Both offer excellent conditions for water lovers. Swimmers, snorkelers and surfers enjoy Hanakaʻōʻō, and Kāʻanapali is good for swimming and beginner windsurfing.

Sugar cane once covered most of Kāʻanapali, and a boat landing for shipping the cane was near the Black Rock area. The Kāʻanapali Resort has made the beach—and Maui—famous.

No fringing reef protects this area, but inshore waters usually are calm; nevertheless, an infrequent storm can cause high waves along the beach. Public access to Hanakaʻōʻō goes through private property here, but many visitors come up the beach from Kāʻanapali. Access to Kāʻanapali is via a public right of way at the north end of the beach.

8 Wahikuli State Wayside Park ★★★ ●●

Breathtaking views and excellent swimming and snorkeling make this one of West Maui's most attractive beach parks. The park's lovely sandy beach and its convenience regularly draw a crowd. There are good facilities, including restrooms, showers, pavilions, grills and picnic tables.

LAHAINA/KĀ'ANAPALI

9 Lahaina ★★ ●●●

Snorkeling, scuba diving and surfing are popular at this beach, which begins at the end of the Boat Harbor and continues along Front Street. A shallow and very rocky bottom between the reef and the beach discourages most swimmers. Paved parking access to the beach is provided.

Soothing Wailea Beach sunset.

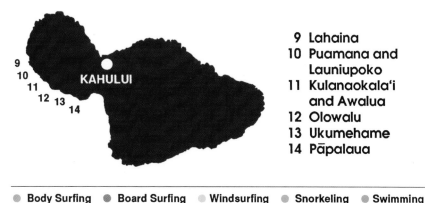

9 Lahaina
10 Puamana and
    Launiupoko
11 Kulanaokalaʻi
    and Awalua
12 Olowalu
13 Ukumehame
14 Pāpalaua

● Body Surfing ● Board Surfing ● Windsurfing ● Snorkeling ● Swimming

10 Puamana Park/Launiupoko State Wayside Park ★★★ ●●

These convenient parks feature sandy beaches, a pleasant atmosphere and large trees. Both beaches have pockets of sand and rock, and Launiupoko has a childrens' wading area next to the beach. The parks include paved parking lots, grills, restrooms and picnic tables.

11 Kulanaokalaʻi and Awalua ★★ ●●

The picturesque view of other islands from these beaches and the easy swimming offshore make this a popular area with visitors. A low spit of sand called 'Cut Mountain' divides the beaches. These are unimproved yet attractive beaches, with easy access but without amenities. The Hawaiian word, Kulanaokalaʻi, translates beautifully: 'to stand firmly in the calmness of the sea'.

12 Olowalu ★ ●●●

This excellent spot for snorkeling and scuba diving also holds an important place in Maui's history. The beach is the site of a famous massacre (see SIGHT-SEEING); today visitors can combine a walk among petroglyphs and the remains of a *heiau* with snorkeling. The swimming is only fair because of the shallow reef offshore.

13 Ukumehame Beach Park ★★ ●●●

This narrow, roadside park is a popular spot among local fishermen. Near the shore, the ocean is shallow and the bottom has patches of sand and rock. There is public access and paved parking at this park.

14 Pāpalaua State Wayside Park ★★ ●●

A long, narrow beach fronts this roadside park and provides a wonderful vantage point for viewing the island of Kahoʻolawe. The offshore ocean bottom is rocky and shallow. The beach has public access, barbecue grills, picnic tables and portable comfort stations.

KĪHEI/WAILEA

15 Mā'alaea ★★ ●●●●●

To the left of this beach is a bird sanctuary, and to the right, a boat harbor. Not an especially good swimming beach, Mā'alaea offers at least two good surfing areas. At times, a strong wind makes this area uncomfortable for picnickers. Maps may show a variety of names for this beach, but they are simply old shoreline names. Fitness buffs know it as a place where they can jog on hard-packed sand, but again, the strong winds here can act as a deterrent. There are no public facilities but there is public access.

16 Maipoina'oeia'u Beach Park ★★★★ ●●●●

The name in Hawaiian means 'do not forget me' and the park is dedicated to "all those who sacrificed their lives to preserve our freedom for all humanity." Consequently, the park also is known as 'Veterans Park', and sometimes as 'Memorial Park'. The beach here is a continuation of the long ribbon of sand that extends along the southwest coast. There is a fine, sandy bottom offshore with only a sprinkling of rocks. Facilities include a paved parking lot, showers, picnic tables and restrooms.

17 Kalama Beach Park ★★★★ ●●●●

This park is as much a playground as a haven for water lovers. Offshore, the bottom is rocky with pockets of sand, but off to the right is a long stretch of sandy beach. The park is huge, with a dozen pavilions along with restrooms, picnic tables, grills, tennis courts, a soccer field—and more.

18 Kama'ole Beach Parks I, II and III ★★★★★ ●●●●

These three separate parks are simply unbeatable for good swimming, sandy beaches, brilliant views and a fine climate. These are among the best beaches in Hawai'i. The only time swimming is not safe is during the occasional storms that come up from the south-southwest, known as kona storms. Facilities are excellent, with paved parking, public access that is clearly marked, showers, grills, picnic tables and restrooms.

19 Wailea ★★★★★ ●●●

Conjure up the ideal shore, and one of these wide, white sand beaches with graceful curves and offshore views of other islands will probably fit the bill. The broad expanse of sand and unbeatable climate make these very attractive spots for sun worshippers and water lovers. There is public access to the four beaches—**Keawakapu**, **Mōkapu**, **Ulua**, and **Wailea**—but no public facilities.

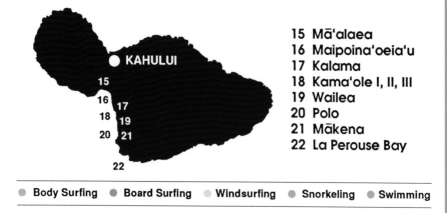

15 Māʻalaea
16 Maipoinaʻoeiaʻu
17 Kalama
18 Kamaʻole I, II, III
19 Wailea
20 Polo
21 Mākena
22 La Perouse Bay

● Body Surfing ● Board Surfing ● Windsurfing ● Snorkeling ● Swimming

20 Polo ★★★ ●●●

Long and wide, Polo Beach is only one of several that make up the Wailea beach area. Snorkelers will enjoy this beach, but should watch for storms or high surf that can cause strong currents. The beach has a small park and a paved parking area but no other public facilities.

21 Mākena ★★★★ ●●●●

These sweeping beaches with beautiful stretches of sand, plenty of room and panoramic views of Molokini and Kahoʻolawe lie more or less adjacent to each other. The beaches of **Poʻolenalena, Maluʻaka, Onouli, Puʻuōlaʻi** and **Oneloa** have good swimming and snorkeling. Board surfing at Puʻuōlaʻi and Oneloa is popular, as is body surfing at all but Onouli. There is a dark sand beach, a rocky offshore bottom and steep drop-off at Onouli. Mākena once had a boat landing for interisland steamers; its future seems destined for resort development because of the excellent beaches and the fine climate. These beaches are reached via the same road that leads back through Wailea and Kīhei. None of the beaches has restrooms or other public facilities.

22 La Perouse Bay ★★ ●●●

Fishermen more than swimmers come to this public beach, where the first non-Hawaiian set foot on Maui. Captain Jean Francois de Galaup, Comte de La Perouse, came ashore on May 30, 1786. La Perouse was one of France's fine navigators and explorers, but when he sailed on into the Pacific his vessel disappeared with all hands, and his fate remains a mystery of the sea. Here at the bay named for him, a series of small beaches lie between rocky out-croppings, and there are many tidal pools. Waters can become rough during storms or heavy surf. There is public access but no facilities at this rocky beach.

Beyond La Perouse Bay the coastline is rugged and dramatic. In general, the beaches of this area are small, remote and lacking in both facilities and public access. Continuing past the pavement violates most car rental

KĪHEI/WAILEA

contracts. Visitors who are able to make their way down to these areas would be wise to admire them without getting into the water. Additionally, there are many scenic shoreline areas before reaching the Nu'u Landing, including the many small inlets that are visible as the road winds down toward the coast from 'Ulupalakua, and the dark sand beach of Huakini Bay.

HĀNA

23 Seven Pools Park ★★★★★ (for its beauty)

The beach itself is dangerous, but the series of beautiful pools below the highway are stunning. There are more than seven pools—actually twenty-four, above and below a bridge. Swimmers should beware of flash flooding and stay out of the area in heavy rainfall. The bridge over 'Ohe'o Stream is a good place to see up and down the Kīpahulu Valley. Hiking and camping in the area are possible but remember: no ocean swimming here, because of the strong currents and the prevalence of sharks. The area has many legends, but for years was erroneously called sacred; today it is a favorite stopping place for visitors.

'Ohe'o Gulch, better known as Seven Pools.

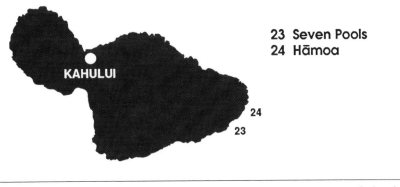

23 Seven Pools
24 Hāmoa

KAHULUI

24

23

● Body Surfing   ● Board Surfing   ● Windsurfing   ● Snorkeling   ● Swimming

24   *Hāmoa Beach* ★★★★ ●●●

This jewel-like setting evokes the idyllic tropical paradise, with its high cliffs and sheer beauty. The good running surf makes this as popular a beach today as it was in earlier times. Breaking surf comes straight into the beach and often creates some strong currents near the shore. At times there is a lifeguard provided by the Hotel Hana-Maui, whose guests frequent the beach. There is public access down a trail from the road, but no public facilities.

Wai'ānapanapa's coarse black sand beach.

HĀNA

25   Hāna Beach Park ★★★ ●●

A favorite of residents and tourists alike, this large, pleasant beach park features good swimming and snorkeling, but some fearsome currents out past the sheltered bay. Nevertheless, the area is safe and generally calm, with shorebreaks and gentle winds. The sand is brown and clean. The park includes a pavilion, picnic tables, restrooms and showers, paved parking and a boat ramp.

26   Wai'ānapanapa State Park ★★★★ ●

This large, scenic and historic park is a good spot for picnicking and swimming—when the water is calm and if you are a strong swimmer. Wai'ānapanapa must be approached with some caution because of strong rip currents and a beach unprotected by any reef. Further along at Pa'iloa, sunbathers and explorers will enjoy the black sand beach. It is easy to spend long hours in this area because of the ancient legends associated with it (see Hāna under SIGHTSEEING), and visitors should plan to bring a lunch and stay a while. The park has excellent facilities, from paved parking to restrooms and picnic areas.

WAILUKU-KAHULUI

27   Lower Nāhiku to Māliko Bay ★ ●●

The coves and inlets along this fascinating but difficult coastline are not good for swimming or other water sports. Board surfing and snorkeling are possible, but public access is difficult to find; there are other places where the water is murky from stream runoff; and still other places where a calm ocean means fishing or just strolling the shoreline. In at least one spot the county of Maui has posted Keep Out signs, because rental cars frequently get stuck. Still, the coastline itself is engaging.

28   Ho'okipa Beach Park ★★★★ ●●● (expert)

This convenient park alongside Hāna Highway is a mecca for windsurfers from all over the world. It is not a great place to swim, but it is the best for windsurfing and can be good for surfing. Ho'okipa is the home of Maui surfing, dating back to the 1930s. This park's high rating comes not for its easy ways, but for its challenge, its claim to the world championship windsurfing site. It is, simply, the best around for what it offers. There are pavilions, showers, grills, restrooms, picnic tables and a paved parking lot.

29   Lower Pā'ia Park ★ ●●●

This is a temperamental area, with good swimming when waters are calm, but poor otherwise. There are shorebreaks for body surfing and offshore breaks

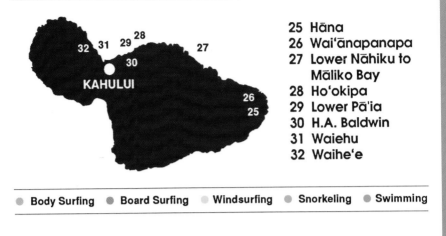

25 Hāna
26 Wai'ānapanapa
27 Lower Nāhiku to Māliko Bay
28 Ho'okipa
29 Lower Pā'ia
30 H.A. Baldwin
31 Waiehu
32 Waihe'e

KAHULUI

● Body Surfing ● Board Surfing ● Windsurfing ● Snorkeling ● Swimming

for board surfing, but these can be quirky. Windsurfers frequent the area. To the right of the park is a rocky point from which local children jump into the water. There are restrooms, picnic areas, a softball field and basketball courts.

30 H.A. Baldwin Park ★★★ ●●●●

Bodysurfers flock to this long sandy beach that probably is the most used beach park in this corner of Maui. The surf breaks along the shore, and occasionally offshore as well, attracting surfers, especially windsurfers. There are excellent facilities: picnic tables, pavilions, grills, restrooms, showers, plus playing fields suitable for soccer and baseball, and plenty of parking. The park is named for Harry A. Baldwin, delegate to Congress and community leader.

Heading out for the challenge of Ho'okipa's wave riding conditions.

WAILUKU-KAHULUI

31   Waiehu Beach Park   ★ ●●

On clear days there is no better place to get a good view of Haleakalā than from this beach park. While the swimming here is poor, the park is a wonderful out-of-the-way spot for a picnic and for viewing the ocean. Parts of this beach are heavily used by local fishermen. The park is next to the Waiehu Municipal Golf Course, and once also contained a wharf that was destroyed in the tsunami of 1946. The park includes a pavilion, restrooms, showers, grills and picnic tables.

32   Waiheʻe Beach Park   ★★ ●●●

An impressive reef creates a good swimming area off this beach park, which forms one boundary of the Waihee Golf Course. However, swimmers must watch for strong currents that occur where the reef ends. Residents come to this beach to gather *limu* [seaweed]. There are restrooms, picnic areas and a paved parking lot. Access is via Halewaiu Road.

SPORTS

Windsurfing
Golfing
Hiking
Whale watching

SPORTS & RECREATION

Maui's climate and terrain combine to make this an outdoor enthusiast's paradise, perfect for the many traditional sports savored for centuries by Hawaiians, as well as more modern-day pursuits. A variety of recreational activities awaits the visitor—some, such as whale watching, can be enjoyed in few other places in the world. You may wish to try one of the sports so synonymous with Hawai'i—like surfing—or something more universal, like golfing. In either case, the conditions and setting are ideal.

To enjoy your Maui recreational experience, use the proper equipment; pay attention to the common-sense rules of safety; and get the necessary permits. Also be on guard in the water, as Maui has few lifeguards along its beaches. The few you will see are employed by the hotels in the area. Maui has no official water rescue units; the people who are likely to assist in water emergencies are volunteers. Swimming, surfing and snorkeling areas are listed under BEACHES.

SCUBA DIVING and SNORKELING

Another world awaits exploration along Maui's shores. Good scuba diving and snorkeling are possible year-round at many spots off Maui for beginning and advanced divers.

Among favorite diving areas are: Wai'ānapanapa State Park, Hāna Bay and Nu'u Landing along the Hāna Coast; Mākena Beach, Hāloa Point, Wailea and Ulua Beaches, and McGregor Point along the Southwest Coast; Olowalu and Black Rock in West Maui; and Kapalua Bay, D.T. Fleming Beach Park, Honolua Bay and Hononana Bay at Kapalua.

One of the most popular dive sites in Hawai'i is Molokini Island, a crescent-shaped top of an eroded volcano, a quick boat ride away from Maui. Exploring its surrounding waters is an experience that many divers repeat as often as possible. Taking any ocean creatures from this marine conservation district is prohibited. As a result, the area is brimming with ocean life, from eels to turtles, from whitetip reef sharks to manta rays. Diving the back side of the island instead of the bay affords a truly spectacular underwater view of the volcano's sharp decline and hints at the depth of surrounding waters. Remember, however, that the back side of Molokini also has strong currents, so caution is advised.

There are a number of shops on Maui that rent scuba and snorkeling equipment and have diving maps. Some of the diving charter companies and retailers also organize whale-watching cruises and photographic tours. Most of them also certify new divers after the required courses, which generally last five days.

Among dive shops in Lahaina are: **Capt. Nemo's** (661-5555); **Central Pacific Divers** (661-8718);

Dive Maui (667-2080); Extended Horizons (667-0611); Hawaiian Reef Divers (667-7647); Lahaina Divers (657-7885) and Sundance Charters (661-4126). Kihei shops include: The Dive Shop (879-5172), Makena Coast Charters (874-1273), Molokini Divers (879-0055) and Ocean Enterprises (879-7067).

Maui Dive Shop operates out of Lahaina (661-5388), Kihei (879-3388/4188), and Kahului (871-2111) and carries beach and water sports accessories of every description.

SURFING

While many Polynesians enjoyed riding the surf in their outrigger canoes, Hawaiians alone developed the art of riding boards specifically designed for play atop the rolling waves. It is not surprising that they invented the sport of surfing, since these island-based people lived constantly within reach of the sea and its changing waves.

In modern times, this ancient sport has been refined and extended beyond anything its inventors ever imagined. Its popularity has spread around the globe, with professional surfers demonstrating their skill and daring while vying for six-figure purses.

The manufacture of surfing equipment and accessories has become a major industry. Several types of board surfing also have developed as well as, in recent years, the new variant: surf sailing or windsurfing. A description of these can be found in *The Essential Guide to O'ahu*.

The areas of Maui best suited to these various types of surfing are noted in the BEACHES section.

"Howzit brah"—the typical pidgin English greeting.

WINDSURFING

Windsurfing is a marriage of surfing and sailing that is even more complicated than it appears because it requires techniques and styles that are being improved all the time. This modern variation of the ancient sport of surfing was conceived by Californian Hoyle Schweitzer in 1970, and executed by his friend Jim Drake. The new sport caught on like wildfire. Today a well-established circuit of amateur and professional contests exists.

On Maui, windsurfing has grown in quantum leaps, and Ho'okipa Beach, on the island's North Coast, has become an internationally recognized site of world windsurfing championships. Windsurfing contributes some $10 million a year to the Maui economy.

Windsurfing schools include: **Kaanapali Windsurfing School** (667-1964), **Maui Windsurf Co.** (877-4816), **Maui Windsurfari** (367-8047), **Paia Beach Center** (579-8000), **Second Wind** (877-7467) and **Windsurfing West** (871-8733) specializing in "beginners and cowards." Most also rent sailboards as do the **Ocean Activities Center** (879-8022/4485) in Wailea and the **Maui Sailing and Activity Center** (879-5935) in Kīhei.

Colorful sails are almost always on display at Ho'okipa.

PARASAILING

Some people prefer to rise above it all—up to 200 feet in a parasail. Power boats tow the parasails and the wind does the rest. The result is a stunning, and different, view of Maui. **West Maui Para-Sail** (661-4060) is one of the older companies around. **Lahaina Para-Sail** (661-4887) and **Parasailing Hawaii** (661-5322) both operate from Lahaina. **UFO Parasailing** (661-7836) is located in Kā'anapali. **Wailea Parasail** (879-1999) operates from the Wailea area.

WATERSKIING and JETSKIING

Lahaina Para-Sail (661-4887) also offers waterski charters for beginners to advanced skiers. **Lahaina Water Ski** (661-5988) is located near the south end of Kā'anapali Beach. **Kaanapali Water Ski** (661-3324) is close by. **Pacific Jet Ski Rentals** (667-2066) rents out of Lahaina.

Parasailing high above West Maui waters.

TENNIS

Maui has approximately eighty tennis courts available for public use, and the island's fine climate means the courts get plenty of use all year long. Some courts are lighted for evening play. Listed here are free public courts and resort or commercial courts available to the public for a fee. Resort courts open to the public offer additional facilities to guests, and racquet rentals are available.

Public courts in the Lahaina/Kā'anapali area include: **Lahaina Civic Center**, two courts, and **Malu'uluoLele Park**, four lighted courts. There are two courts at **Kalama Park** in Kīhei, and two lighted and three grass courts at **Hāna Ball Park**. In Upcountry, the **Eddie Tam Center** in Makawao and the **Community Center** in **Pukalani** both have two courts. In the Wailuku-Kahului region, courts include: the **Community Center** in Kahului, two lighted courts; the **Community Center** in **Wailuku**, seven courts; **Maui Community College**, four courts; and **Maui War Memorial**, four courts.

Resort and commercial courts in the Kapalua area include: **Kapalua Tennis Garden** (669-5677), ten plexi-pave courts, four of them lighted. In Lahaina/Kā'anapali, courts are located at: **Maui Marriott Resort Tennis Shop** (667-1200), five courts; **Royal Lahaina Tennis Ranch** (661-3611), eleven courts, six of them lighted, pro shop, instruction, rentals; and **Sheraton-Maui Hotel Tennis Courts** (661-0031), three lighted courts. In Kīhei/Wailea, courts are found at: **Makena Tennis Club** (879-8777), six plexi-pave courts, pro shop and snack bar; **Maui Sunset** (879-0674), two unlighted courts; and **Wailea Tennis Center** (879-1958), eleven hard-surface courts, three of them lighted, and three grass courts, plus pro shop, lessons and rentals.

GOLFING

From duffer to professional, there's no golf like golf in Maui. The courses are different in design and difficulty, but they share vivid scenery and beautiful climate. The courses listed here are open to the public; green fees are competitive with courses elsewhere, but rates can vary considerably from summer to winter, with winter prices being higher.

Royal Kaanapali Golf Courses (661-3691, 667-7111) helped bring championship golf to Maui when they were first opened. The two courses have excellent views of the ocean and the West Maui Mountains. The North Course is a Robert Trent Jones design; at one point the ocean is a water hazard, and Kā'anapali Beach is a sand trap. This is an 18-hole, par 72 (forward tees par 73) course. The South Course was designed by Arthur Jack Snyder and is 18 holes, par 72. The fourth hole sometimes offers a distraction as the Sugarcane Train chugs by. The Courses feature a pro shop, rentals, storage, lessons and a restaurant.

Kapalua Golf Club (669-8044) must be ranked among the most beautiful in Hawai'i—or anywhere else. There are two courses. The Bay Course is 18 holes, par 72, and has two ocean holes; the course was designed by Arnold Palmer. The Village Course is 18 holes, par 71, and designed by Arnold Palmer and Ed Seay. This course offers panoramic views; the 18th green is bordered by a lake. They also have fine amenities, including two pro shops, club rentals and storage, golf lessons, restaurants and bar, putting greens and a driving range.

Wailea Golf Course (879-2966) boasts incredible weather and sweeping views. There are two courses. The Blue Course is 18 holes, par 72, and, like the companion Orange Course, was designed by Arthur Jack Snyder. On the Blue Course golfers encounter two lakes and a fair number of hills. On the Orange Course, 18 hole, par 72, golfers find tricky greens and hazards that include old stone walls and a lava formation. Pro shop, rentals, lessons and putting greens are available.

Makena Golf Course (879-3344) in Kīhei is an 18-hole, par 72 course

located near the Maui Prince Hotel with sweeping views of Haleakalā and the sea. Robert Trent Jones designed it; amenities include a pro shop, club rentals and two practice putting greens.

The newly landscaped **Silversword Golf Course** (874-0777) located on Pi'ilani Highway in Kīhei is a challenging 18-hole, par 71 course with good rates. The driving range, pro shop, restaurant and bar add to the Course's appeal.

Pukalani Country Club (572-1314) affords a vista of Central Valley and West Maui Mountains, and sometimes strong winds. It is 18 holes, par 72. There is a restaurant at the 18th hole, a pro shop and club rentals.

Waiehu Municipal Golf Course (243-7400) near Wailuku is a fairly difficult 18-hole, par 72 course. The front nine were designed in 1929, the back nine in 1968. There is a pro shop, club and cart rentals.

Maui Country Club (877-0616) in Pā'ia is open to the public only on Mondays. The course has plenty of trees and sometimes gusty winds. It is 9 holes, par 74.

HIKING

At least two dozen trails lead hikers into Maui's beautiful and varied wilderness, those in Haleakalā being the most popular. Trails elsewhere are as short as a half mile and as long as ten to twelve miles, and appeal to different levels of stamina, skill and experience. Besides referring to books about hiking in Hawai'i in RECOMMENDED READING, several local organizations regularly schedule group hiking activities, welcome visitors to join their excursions, and

are happy to provide tips for making your hike pleasant and safe. The most logical procedure for would-be hikers is to inquire with County, State or National park officials for information. Also, some other sources of information include the **Hawaii Geographic Society** (Honolulu 538-3952), PO Box 1698, Honolulu 96806; the **Hawaii Sierra Club** (Honolulu 946-8494), PO Box 11070, Honolulu 96828; or the **Hawaii Trail and Mountain Club**, PO Box 2238, Honolulu 96814.

Hike Maui (879-5270), P.O. Box 330969, Kahului, Hawaii, conducts half-day and full-day hikes for a fee that includes pickup, transportation, equipment and lunch.

Planning and taking safety precautions is especially important when hiking in Haleakalā, which can be difficult if hikers are not equipped properly. Weather conditions in the crater can sometimes change not merely day by day, but hour by hour (see SIGHT-SEEING).

For relatively easy outings, hikers should go along **Halemau'u Trail** from the highway not quite a mile to the rim of the crater, which affords a good view; or down **Sliding Sands Trail**. More difficult, but exciting, is the eight-mile hike down **Halemau'u Trail** to the Hōlua cabin, a trek that takes roughly a half day for an experienced hiker. Good hikers should allow at least eight hours for another expedition: down Sliding Sands Trail to the crater floor, across **KamoaoPele Trail** to Halemau'u Trail, and back to the highway via Hōlua and the Halemau'u Trail.

There are longer hikes, more demanding and more rewarding. One is the hike down Sliding Sands Trail, which includes an overnight stay at Hōlua cabin campground. Another is a hike to Palikū campground for an overnight stay and a return via the Halemau'u Trail.

There are points of interest along the way in the crater. One is the **Bottomless Pit** of the Halemau'u Trail, a ten-foot-wide yawning well that—bottomless or not—is clogged with debris sixty to seventy feet down. Be careful approaching the edge.

The **Bubble Cave** is another point of interest and is not far from the Kapalaoa cabin; it is a large, collapsed bubble made by gases from molten lava in an eruption. The lush, green area around the Palikū cabin sharply contrasts with the desert-like crater floor. **Silversword Loop** off Halemau'u Trail has a number of places that may look like piles of stone, but are the remains of sacred sites constructed by the Hawaiians, and should not be disturbed.

The silversword, a rare plant that dots the crater, is found in few other places and long has been identified with Haleakalā. It is a fragile plant and its roots can be easily damaged if stepped on.

The Park Service asks that all hikers register at the head of each trail heading into the crater. This is a sensible procedure designed to protect the hikers in the event of emergencies.

Another hike begins at the summit and ends some five hours later and nearly 4000 feet down on the outside of Haleakalā. **Skyline Trail** starts at the south end of the Science City complex near the park boundary, leads across a rugged landscape that has a compensating tremendous view, then drops down into scrub trees. Halfway down the trail is a marker pointing to **Haleakalā Ridge Trail**. A third of a mile in that direction the **Polipoli Trail** branches off and leads to Polipoli Springs State Recreational Area. This tough but rewarding hike ends in the midst of magnificent hardwood trees.

It is important to remember that no matter how warm it may seem at sea level, the temperatures get markedly cooler—as much as thirty degrees—in the higher elevations of Haleakalā, whether inside the crater or out. Warm clothing and raingear are necessary. If you intend to cook at the campgrounds inside the crater it is necessary to bring in a lightweight grid or cookstove. Open wood fires are not permitted.

Below Polipoli there are a number of connected trails— **Redwood**, **Boundary**, **Polipoli**, **Tie** and **Plum**. **Waiohuli Trail**, tying up with Boundary Trail, leads to an overlook with a view of Kēōkea, a small Kula community, and on to Kīhei on Maui's Southwest Coast. **Waiakoa Trail** begins at the Kula Forest Reserve and winds seven miles up Haleakalā and comes back through a series of dramatic switchbacks. This network of trails offers spectacular views, and close-

hikes. All offer close-up views of the profuse plants and flowers. No permission is necessary to hike any of these well-marked trails.

One 'Īao Valley trail begins behind the lookout shelter and winds through the bluff and back to the parking lot; this is **Tableland Trail**, about two hours and two miles long, and relatively strenuous. Equally challenging, but rewarding, is the three-mile **Po'ohahoahoa Stream hike**, which should be taken by only the most physically fit and experienced hikers.

In the southwestern area of Maui, a six-mile trek on the **King's Highway Trail** through the 1790 lava flow is a popular hike. It

Hiking up in the clouds at Haleakalā Crater.

ups of the wide variety of Maui flora.

Back in the Central Valley, the beautiful park area of 'Īao Valley near Wailuku is crisscrossed by trails demanding different levels of expertise. There are easy walks for the family, and more demanding

begins at La Perouse Bay and goes south and inland, ending eventually on private property. Around the coast and back in the Hāna area, the **Wai'ānapanapa Trail** begins at the park and follows the old King's Highway path over a trail that is well defined, but not gentle.

SPORTS & RECREATION

Horseback riding, an alternative to hiking the Crater.

HORSEBACK RIDING

Some of the most spectacular riding trails in the world cross Maui pastures, woodlands and lava flows. Excursions range from pleasant and uncomplicated rides, to overnight expeditions into Haleakalā Crater. Riding a horse along a sandy beach or past an old Hawaiian *heiau*, into the crater or along a high meadow, is a great experience on Maui. There are stables on Maui that offer lessons to novices, in preparation for later rides that may be extended—and more challenging. **Equine Farms of Maui** (572-9544) offers training and instruction in dressage and jumping. **Makawao Town and Country Stables** (572-0788) is in a cool, Upcountry location, as is the **Mauka-lani Riding School** (572-0606), which offers discounts to senior citizens. The stables listed here are specifically geared to handle riding excursions:

East Maui—**Charles Aki, Jr** (248-8209) in Kaupō arranges overnight trips into Haleakalā Crater, with stays either at the cabins or the campgrounds. **Pony Express Tours** (667-2200) of Makawao can manage overnight or day-long crater trips, and like Charles Aki, provides equipment and food as well as guide. **Thompson Ranch Riding Stables** (878-1910) in Kula is closed on Tuesday but otherwise can handle a variety of riding plans. On the Hāna Coast, **Hotel Hana-Maui** (248-8211) conducts guided riding tours of the sprawling Hāna Ranch; non-guests are invited, but on a space-available basis.

Southeast Maui—**Makena Stable** (879-0244) in Kīhei has hourly rentals, plus guided rides over 'Ulupalakua Ranch land.

West Maui—Lahaina's **Rainbow Ranch Riding Stables** (669-4991) offers a wide variety of rides, and provides instruction in both Western and English-style horsemanship. **Kaanapali Kau Lio** (667-7896) arranges free pickup at Kā'anapali resorts, and on five-hour rides, offers a ranch barbecue.

HUNTING

Maui has considerable State land where hunting is permitted to those with licenses. Feral pigs, goats, pheasant and francolin are the game. Hunters should go in person to the proper State office and pick up both hunting regulations and maps of the proscribed areas. The office is the State of Hawai'i, Department of Land and Natural Resources, Division of Forestry and Wildlife, State Office Building, 54 High Street, Wailuku 96793 (244-4352). Most of the hunting area is in East Maui. Hunting seasons generally last from November through January, but it is best to check with the Forestry and Wildlife office. In addition to the State Office Building, licenses can be obtained at Honsport (877-3954), a retail store in Kahului's Kaahumanu Center, or from AA Go Go Bikes Hawaii (661-3063) in Kā'anapali. Persons who bring firearms into Hawai'i must register them with local police within twenty-four hours or face a penalty. If guns are rented or purchased here, they also must be registered with police.

Hunting on private lands is next to impossible on Maui unless you are acquainted with persons who own property on which they will allow you to hunt. In that eventuality, other State regulations, such as registration of guns, may still apply and it is a good idea to discuss the proposed hunting with the State's Division of Forestry and Wildlife.

SAILING and FISHING

Recreational ocean fishing along Maui's shoreline does not require a license, and there is no freshwater fishing here. Opinions on the best fishing areas are like other fish tales—they vary with the telling. Experienced fishermen soon learn to talk with the owners of sporting goods stores to get a fix on the best fishing spots.

With the Pacific as a playground, it is no wonder that Maui spawns numerous charter boats for hire. Some of them are simply for cruising, some for deep-sea fishing only. Still others advertise sailing and snorkeling trips, or fishing-snorkeling-picnic sails. The boats range from serviceable dive boats to luxurious fifty-eight-foot catamarans. Many of the boats for charter also take trips to Molokini Island, the collapsed volcano that now has

a sweeping half-moon bay and is a marine conservation area. Hotel desks have the latest information on the various types of charters, plus the latest fees.

Although the 'Big Island' of Hawai'i is the mecca for fishermen, Maui is justly famous for its game fishing. Record-breaking *a'u* [marlin] have been pulled from local waters, and on a day-to-day basis, fishermen take on the *'ahi* [yellowfin tuna], *aku* [skipjack tuna], *mahimahi* [dolphin fish], *ono* [wahoo], and *ulua* [jack crevalle]. The blue marlin can run larger than a thousand pounds and sailfish, more than 200 pounds. The *mahimahi* and the tuna are strong fighting fish, a thrill to hook.

Most fishing boats come back with a catch, and one operator guarantees fish on his bottom-fishing expedition or you get the next fishing trip free. It is customary to tip the skipper and crew after a successful voyage, or perhaps offer to share the fish.

Most of the deep-sea fishing is done in calm waters on the lee side of Maui; this also affords good views of other islands. Many of the boats have sounders that make sonar sweeps for schools of fish; one has an additional offering—a Hawaiian storyteller who recites ancient legends as the boat sails home.

Here is a sampling of local boats for charter: **The Pacific Whale Foundation** (879-8811) at 101 N Kīhei Road, Kīhei, operates a cruise/snorkel research boat, fifty-three-foot *Whale One*, to select snorkeling areas; provides the storyteller coming home; and also provides all equipment. *Excel* (877-3333) at Slip 61, Mā'alaea Harbor, guarantees fish or your next trip free when bottom fishing. The three-

masted schooner *Spirit of Wind-jammer* (661-8600) offers a two-hour sunset sail with open bar, meal and Polynesian show, and operates from Slip 1 at Lahaina. *The Coral See* (661-8600) operates from Slip 1 at Lahaina, and is a sixty-five-foot glass-bottom boat specializing in Molokini snorkel and picnic cruises. **Lahaina Charter Boats** (667-6672) operates the *Broadbill* and the *Judy Ann*, and offers group rates. At Slip 2 in Lahaina is the *Scotch Mist* (661-0386), which features a champagne sunset sail, plus snorkeling. One of the island's most beautiful boats, the *Lavengro* (879-8177), is a classic schooner operated by **Maui Classic Charters**. *The Genesis* (667-5667) is an Irwin ketch which offers snorkel cruises or sailing, and operates from the Lahaina dock.

Double-hulled canoes are a Pacific tradition that have evolved into modern catamarans. **Alihilani Yacht Charters** (661-3047) operates two catamarans, the *Makani Wiki*, a thirty-six foot McGregor catamaran, and the original ocean-racing *Aikane*, a forty-six footer. The service will sail you over to the island of Lāna'i and stop for snorkeling off Halepalaoa Landing, where there is a lively coral reef.

Aerial Sportfishing Charters (667-9089) and **Between the Sheets** (661-4095) both sail out of Lahaina, the former on fishing excursions, the latter for snorkeling or cruising. Also in Lahaina, **Capt. Nemo's Ocean Emporium** (661-5555) offers a good variety of cruises, from sailing to Lāna'i to snorkeling, scuba diving or sunset sails. They operate the fifty-eight-foot catamaran *Seasmoke*.

Inflatable rafts are another way of plying Maui's waters. **Captain**

Zodiac (667-5351) sails out of Lahaina in twenty-three-foot Zodiacs. **Pardner Charters** (661-3448) and **Lucky Strike Charters** (661-4606) are experienced in seeking out deep-water fish, and the latter offers bottom fishing as well.

Cruises can be booked and tailored to satisfy your particular interests at: **Ocean Activities Center** in Wailea (879-4485) and Lahaina (661-5309); and **Tom Barefoot's Cashback Tours** (661-8889) also in Lahaina.

Most whale-watching excursions depart from Lahaina Harbor.

WHALE WATCHING

The North Pacific humpback whales have been popular attractions in the Islands since 1966. But they have plied Hawaiian waters for much longer, though no one is sure for how long. Some scientists believe the mammals have been here for centuries. Others say there is little evidence that they were here more than 200 years ago.

There is no doubt, however, that Hawaiian waters became dangerous territory for whales in 1819 when two whaling ships, *The Balaena* and *The Equator*, became the first of

hundreds to make port here. Maui became the whaling capital of the Pacific, the place for reprovisioning, rest and recreation.

The whaling industry gave rise to at least five shore-based whaling stations by the late 1860s. They disappeared a decade later, the humpbacks hunted to the very edge of extinction and the industry doomed.

Today whales still face dangers, but are showing signs of recovery. Whale watching, meanwhile, has become a new industry in itself.

Local organizations began to focus on scientific study of the migrating whales. The motivation to protect the large mammal grew appreciably. The International Whaling Commission scored an impressive victory when a moratorium on commercial whaling was passed in 1982. In 1987 the commission closed a loophole through which some whaling nations were able to take up to 1500 whales a year for 'scientific purposes'. Japan announced it would end its Southern Ocean minke whaling and its hunting of bryde's whales, and in 1988 ended its coastal sperm whaling. Still, uncounted numbers of whales—along with dolphins, seals and birds—die by entanglement in fishing nets each year. Some fear that certain whales will be taken prematurely from the endangered species list. Some whale aficionados are pushing for implementation of a 'management and recovery plan' for the humpbacks.

When the whales arrive in Maui waters (see The Whales under the INTRODUCTION) most of Maui's charter boats become instant whale-watching platforms. The boats simply add this recreation to their other specialties, and/or run special whale-watching expeditions. To protect the whales from harassment, though, no boats are allowed to get extremely close to the whales, or to come between a whale and her calf. Similarly, helicopters and aircraft have strict height limits so as not to disturb the magnificent mammals while they are in the Hawaiian breeding grounds. Boat skippers know and respect the necessity of keeping a little distance and cannot be persuaded to go any closer than the regulation distance; currently this is no closer than 300 yards in the Māʻalaea Bay or Olowalu areas, or a hundred yards in the open ocean.

Photographing the whales from a distance with ordinary camera lenses is difficult, but much improved if using an 80-200 zoom lens. The whales that breach—leap almost out of the water—tend to do it more than once, affording great photo possibilities. If you see the tail flukes go high in the air, the whale is heading for a deep dive, will be down ten to fifteen minutes, and then come up somewhere else. Whale watching, enhanced greatly by using binoculars, can be done from a roadside park or scenic point, from the air or by boat.

HEALTH CLUBS

Most local health clubs welcome visitors, and most are open seven days a week. Here are some major ones: **Lahaina Health Club** (667-6684) on Kāʻanapali Beach; **Lahaina Nautilus Center** (667-6100) 180 Dickenson St., Ste. 201, Lahaina; **World Gym** (874-0101), 1325 S Kīhei Road, Kīhei; **Powerhouse** **Gym Maui** (879-1326) 1325 So. Kīhei Rd., Kīhei; **Nautilus World** (244-3244) at 1325 Lower Main Street, Wailuku; and **Valley Isle Fitness Center** (242-6851), Wailuku Industrial Park. Most clubs have up-to-date equipment, conduct aerobics classes, and offer supervised programs.

ENTERTAINMENT

Lu'au
Hawaiian music
Social drinking
Calendar of events

ENTERTAINMENT and NIGHTLIFE

For an overwhelming majority of visitors, an evening spent enjoying the lovely Hawaiian ballad, the exciting hula, and the tropical feast is as much a part of a holiday in Maui as a trip to the beach during the day. A Polynesian show or a lu'au is on almost every first-time visitor's agenda, and most seek out Hawaiian music, knowing they're not likely to find it anywhere else. This section outlines the entertainment scene on Maui in general. For specifics, check the free tourist publications and newspapers, magazines and radio stations.

POLYNESIAN SHOWS and LU'AU

The 'Polynesian Show' has become a centerpiece for tourist entertainment on nearly every island in the Pacific Ocean, Polynesian or not. These shows stage performances based on the traditional music, dance and costumes of Hawai'i, Tahiti, Sāmoa, New Zealand and, occasionally, Tonga and the Cook Islands. They are glitzy, show-biz interpretations, and the Tahitian *tamure* invariably highlights the evening with its fast-paced hip-swiveling, grass skirts, tall headdresses and wildly beating drums. Another show-stopper is the Samoan fire dance or its close kin, the knife dance. The shows typically feature the modern—or *'auana*—Hawaiian hula, though some include a traditional *'ōlapa* or *kahiko* hula as well. The Maori (New Zealand) contributions are always a *poi* dance (*poi* in Maori is the white balls on string that the women manipulate so expertly in some of their dances), and the fierce *haka* where men challenge each other (and their audience) with spears and protruding tongues.

Often combined with the Polynesian Show, the most famous feast on your entertainment menu is undoubtedly the lu'au. This Polynesian custom resembles the American Thanksgiving meal, except that the lu'au can be given at any time, for any reason. One good, traditional reason for a lu'au is to honor and entertain visitors, so your attendance at one is entirely appropriate. The feast is named after the taro tops [*lū'au*] that are always served. Usually cooked with coconut cream, they are delectable and unreservedly recommended. Other traditional fare on such occasions includes dishes like *laulau*, small packages of fish, pork, chicken or beef, often with taro tops, wrapped in ti or banana leaves and baked; *poi*, a thick, purplish paste made from the cooked and pounded base of the taro plant (the staple starch food of the Hawaiians); *kālua* pig, traditionally cooked in an underground oven [*imu*]; and *haupia*, thick, creamy coconut pudding.

Though the focus of this feast is food, a lu'au includes a host of entertainment to feed the eye and ear as well. Music, dance, and usually a bit of comedy enhance the festive atmosphere and add to the fun.

A great Polynesian revue called **Drums of the Pacific** takes place at the Hyatt Regency Maui (667-7474), in Kā'anapali. Here the entertainers also take you on a tour through the exotic islands of the Pacific, in a setting of palm trees with the surf not far away. There are shows nightly except Sundays and Thursdays, and you can have your choice of the dinner or the cocktail show, the latter being less costly.

In Wailea, the Maui Intercontinental (879-1922) holds **Maui's Merriest Luau** every Thursday in the Luau Gardens, with poi-pounding and coconut-husking demonstrations starting in the early evening. Following the lu'au, a fire dancer twirls flaming knives in a fast-paced show that includes songs and dances from around the Pacific.

At the Aston Maui Lu Resort (879-5881), the Saturday night **Maui Lu Luau**, focuses more on the food than the entertainment. Warm local smiles from graceful hula dancers give the audience a satisfying glimpse back into old Hawai'i. In Kā'anapali, the Sheraton-Maui (661-5828) offers the **Aloha Luau** followed by a Polynesian show, Sunday through Thursday nights; the location is Whalers Village, in the heart of the Kā'anapali resort area.

Stouffer Wailea Beach Resort's **Show of Aloha** features a firedancer and Tahitian dancers on Mondays. The lu'au is more traditional, and includes an interesting *imu* ceremony—the presentation of a baked pig. Dancers also perform traditional or *kahiko* hula.

A good lu'au that's small and more traditional is the **Old Lahaina Lu'au** (667-1998). It's held on Mondays, Tuesdays, Thursdays and Saturdays in the early evening. Both the food and the Hawaiian dancing are more authentic than the other show-biz Polynesian revues. The lu'au is held on the beach in Lahaina.

The **Royal Lahaina Luau**, held at the Royal Lahaina Resort in Kā'anapali (661-3611), features a spectacular Polynesian revue, along with a dinner buffet and open bar. They stage one show per night, every night. The **Hawaiian Country Barbeque & Revue** (244-7643) held Mondays, Wednesdays and Fridays at Maui Tropical Plantation in Wailuku has, in addition to a generous buffet, a Hawaiian Country Revue that blends Polynesian song and dance with country music.

HULA

If a lu'au epitomizes the culinary delights of our island culture, hula captures its heartbeat. Dance was an integral part of the rituals observed by ancient Hawaiians, and the old hula never died. New dances evolved, and became popular entertainment for visiting sailors. Today, both the old and new hula are performed.

Hula 'ōlapa, more recently known as *hula kahiko*, is the old style, and is performed to accompanying chanting and percussion only.

While most hula groups—or *hālau*—have more women than men performers, the men's hula is every bit as beautiful. It is energetic, with an exciting virile grace. The women's hula is softer, but still has strength and precision, which is a vital element of this hula style.

Hula 'auana, the modern style, is more flexible than the traditional dance. Modern hula usually is accompanied by songs, ukuleles, guitars and other instruments, and the performers' costumes are limited only by their imagination and the stories being told by the dance. Interestingly, the most famous symbol of the hula, the grass skirt, is not Hawaiian at all. The costume was introduced from Micronesia by laborers from the Gilbert Islands in the early nineteenth century. Hawaiians subse-quently used native materials, such as ti leaves, in similar fashion.

Pa'u O Hi'iaka is among several Maui *hālau* that perform both the modern and traditional hula; this troupe specializes in the latter. **Ka Makani Wili Makaha O Kauaula** specializes in the traditional hula, and occasionally performs at Stouffer Wailea Beach Resort. **Pukalani Hula Hale** is another good *hālau* from Pukalani that performs both *kahiko* and *'auana* style of dance. **Halau Hula O Ka'ula** performs Hula Kahiko O Hawai'i, "the ancient dance of Hawai'i," for free at the Kapalua Shops once a week. Maui historian Inez Ashdown contributes Hawaiian legends to the show. Check tourist publications and the *Maui News* for listings of where other hula performances are scheduled.

HAWAIIAN MUSIC

There is no sound more clearly associated with the tropical beauty of these islands than the lovely Hawaiian melody accompanied by the 'ukulele. Such music did not exist in Hawai'i before European contact, and it was the Portuguese laborers who brought the small stringed instrument to these shores in 1879. The steel guitar, played horizontally with a metal slide, is the other stringed instrument linked with our Island music.

Modern Hawaiian music has evolved into many varieties and become less stereotypical in its sound and presentation. *The Essential Guide to O'ahu* details many local musicians, mostly resident on that island but famous statewide. In addition to entertainment listed above under Polynesian Shows and Lū'au, other opportunities to hear Hawaiian music are available. **The Waiehu Sons** are a well-known Hawaiian trio that performs in the Sunset Terrace at Stouffer Wailea Beach Resort (879-4900) Mondays through Fridays. **Hapa**, a guitar-playing duo, performs at El Crab Catcher Restaurant (661-4423) at Whalers Village in Kā'anapali, Thursday through Saturday nights. Hawaiian music is performed during afternoon cocktails by **Windsong** at the Maui Marriott (667-1200) Poolside Bar daily.

Another good source of Hawaiian music is KPOA, 93.5 FM on the radio dial. Also, check the 'Night Beat' column by Jon Woodhouse in the *Maui News* for who is playing where.

CLUBS

West Maui's major resorts always have entertainers to amuse their guests. Nevertheless, club acts come and go, and the most reliable indicator of what's playing at the moment is the daily newspaper. Stroll down Lahaina's Front Street and tune in on the music floating out from the various clubs. Occasionally a well-known entertainer will come to Maui from Honolulu, but these appearances are sporadic. Also, celebrities visiting Maui sometimes stop in at a club and make an unannounced appearance, treating lucky audiences while enhancing the club's reputation.

Willie Nelson did the honors one night after dinner at a restaurant-cum-saloon in Pā'ia called **Charley P. Woofer's** (579-9453). A year or so earlier Ringo Starr polished off a pizza, then jumped up on stage and performed for an enthusiastic, appreciative audience. At **Longhi's** (667-2288) on Lahaina's Front Street, Jimmy Buffett and Johnny Rivers have emerged from the audience for impromptu performances. Longhi's regularly hosts rock and roll bands on Friday and Saturday nights.

Currently, on Fridays and Saturdays you can enjoy jazz at **Blackie's** (667-7979) in Lahaina. You will hear rock and roll at **Moose McGillycuddy's** (667-7758) on Lahaina's Front Street. Disco reigns at **Spats** in the Hyatt Regency Maui (667-7474) from 10pm on, in one of the most spectacularly decorated emporiums on Maui. Similar sounds can be heard at **Banana Moon** in the Maui Marriott (667-1200) from the mid evening on.

At the **Whale's Tale** (661-3676) on Front Street, pianist Chuck Miller takes listeners back to the music of the 1950s Sunday and Monday. Nostalgia buffs often turn up and sing along.

At the Stouffer Wailea Beach Resort (879-4900), a versatile band—playing everything from rock and roll to Hawaiian music—called Hauula packs in Maui residents for dancing and listening past midnight in a tropical setting called **Lost Horizon**.

Wailea's Maui Inter-Continental (879-1922) offers a spicy selection of dancing music in the **Inu Inu Lounge**, open till 1am, Mondays through Saturdays. Bands playing there range in musical styles from jazz to swing to Top-40, and they change frequently.

A live band can always be found at Sheraton-Maui Hotel's (661-0031) **On the Rock** dancing club. **Casanova's** (572-0220) in Makawao has live music Friday and Saturday, disco on Wednesday and Thursday and live jazz on Tuesdays.

ENTERTAINMENT

CHAMBER MUSIC

It is possible to hear chamber music on Maui, but this usually means attendance at a function, such as a convention, where the few practitioners on Maui have been hired to play. Mary Allton (244-7580) can arrange concerts by these musicians.

In the early evening a chamber music group plays in the courtyard of the new **Maui Prince Hotel** (874-1111) in Mākena.

VISITING ARTISTS

Most performers come to Maui to relax, and the majority of them do just that. Now and then an entertainer will be booked into a specific time slot for a certain event, as violinist **Itzak Perlman** has done for the Kapalua Music Festival. The same festival booked the **Tokyo String Quartet**, considered one of the best in the world. Jazzman **Dave Brubeck** has performed on Maui, and a **Willie Nelson** concert in Wailuku resulted in one of the few traffic tie-ups in East Maui.

CINEMA

There are two movie theatres located in Kahului: the Maui Theatre (877-3560) in Kahului Center and Village Cinema (877-6622) in Kaahu-manu Center. In Lahaina, Lahaina Cinemas (661-3347) located on Front Street in the Wharf, has three theatres.

Peaceful day's end, Kā'anapali.

THEATRE

Maui Community Theatre is an active Thespian group that has done at least six productions a year. Its headquarters is located at 68 N Market Street, in Wailuku (242-6969). The group performs in historic Iao Theatre (same address) and is helping to restore it. Maui Community Theatre stages a variety of productions—musicals, drama and comedy. The group also offers discounts for senior citizens.

The Maui Academy of Performing Arts (formerly the Maui Youth Theatre) (871-7484) is a growing organization that stages several plays per year of family entertainment; some are children's shows and many others involve children. In existence since 1974, its educational programs on creative dramatics and theatre art skills are strongly supported in the community.

The Maui Community and Cultural Center (871-8422) is currently being planned with an estimated mid-1992 opening date. It will include visual, performing and literary arts.

The daily newspaper, tourist publications and hotel desks can provide information about both groups' current productions.

SOCIAL DRINKING

After a day of sightseeing or frolicking at the beach, pick out a place to relax with a drink in a quiet setting, preferably one with a view. They, along with livelier alternatives for late evenings are as follows:

Peaceful lounges quiet enough for conversation count in **Pineapple Hill** (669-6129) in Kapalua; the **Sunset Terrace** at Stouffer Wailea Beach Resort (879-4900); **The Chart House** (661-0937) on Front Street; the lounge of **Makawao Steak & Fish House** (572-8711) and **Kihei Prime Rib House** (879-1954); **Buzz's Wharf** (244-5426) at Mā'alaea Harbor; the **Weeping Banyan Bar** of the Hyatt Regency Kā'anapali (667-7474); **The Molokini Lounge** of the Maui Prince Hotel (847-1111), where you can listen to the chamber music mentioned above; and the **Makai Bar** at Maui Marriott Resort (667-1200).

For livelier crowds and louder surroundings, go to **Dillon's** (579-9113) in Pā'ia, where Maui residents frequent to drink and dance; **The Red Dragon** at the Maui Beach Hotel (877-0051) in Kahului; the **Whale's Tale** (661-3676) in Lahaina; and the Maui Marriott's **Banana Moon**. On Friday and Saturday nights there is live entertainment and dancing at **Longhi's** (667-2288) in Lahaina, from 10pm on.

The island's favorite happy hour haunts are **La Familia** (879-8824) and **Rainbow Lagoon Restaurant** (879-5600), both located in Kīhei. Two other places in Kīhei, **Island Fish House** (879-7771) and **Chuck's Steak House** (879-4488) consistently draw crowds.

Polli's Restaurant & Cantina (572-7808) in Makawao and **Polli's on the Beach** (879-5275) in Kīhei have the best margaritas in Hawai'i according to loyal patrons.

The sun's dimming light marks the beginning of a romantic evening.

CALENDAR OF EVENTS

ENTERTAINMENT

JANUARY

January-March

Marine Art Festival—art tours, whale watching tours, sculpture and other demonstrations. Lahaina Gallery, Lahaina 667-7795

FEBRUARY

Asahi Beer Kyosan Golf Tournament—professional men and women golfers from Japan and Hawai'i vie for $100,000 purse. Wailea Golf Course—Blue 879-4465

February-March

Maui Marine Art Expo—artwork from well-known marine artists in an exhibition that gives a portion of the proceeds to the Cousteau Society. Maui Inter-Continental Wailea 879-1922

MARCH

Maui Marathon—annual marathon (26.2 miles) from Maui Mall, Kahului, to Whalers Village, Kā'anapali. 242-8245

APRIL

Art Maui—an annual juried exhibition of works by Maui's art community, 10am-5pm daily during event. Hui Noeau Visual Arts Center, Makawao 572-6560

Grand Masters Tennis Tournament—competition between national or world title winners; also one day of pro am doubles tennis. Hyatt Regency Maui, Kā'anapali 667-7474

Maui Community College Ho'olaule'a—some of Hawai'i's best entertainers perform. Also food booths, arts and crafts and games. Maui Community College, Wailuku 242-1260

Marui O'neill Invitational—first windsurfing event of US Pro Tour. Features 150 competitors from sixteen countries vying for $30,000 prize money. Ho'okipa Beach, Pā'ia. Ehman Productions 579-9765

Buddha Day—flower festival pageant at island temples statewide to celebrate the birth of Buddha. Hawaii Buddhist Council 538-3805 (Honolulu). Sweet tea ceremony, flower presentation, fun day for kids (races and balloons), lunch and bingo games. Lahaina Jodo Mission 661-0640

Royal Lahaina Open—part of Hawai'i Grand Prix series with the biggest prize money of the series, $6,000. Royal Lahaina Tennis Ranch, Kā'anapali 661-3611 x2296

ENTERTAINMENT

108

CALENDAR OF EVENTS

MAY

May Day/Lei Day Celebration—island-wide lei-making contest; Hawaiian entertainment and crafts. Maui Inter-Continental Wailea 879-1922 x227

Seabury Hall Craft Fair—arts and crafts, food booths, games and entertainment. Seabury Hall, Makawao 572-7235

Kapalua Tennis Jr. Vet/Sr. Championship—men and women thirty-five years and older compete in singles, doubles and mixed doubles. Cocktail party included. Kapalua Tennis Garden 669-5677

Hal "Aku" Lewis Golf and Tennis Tournament—Hollywood celebrities participate in this tournament for charity. Maui Inter-Continental Wailea. 879-4465

JUNE

King Kamehameha Celebration—state holiday honoring Kamehameha the Great. Celebration on all islands. State Council on Hawaiian Heritage 536-6540 (Honolulu). On Maui—parade in Lahaina, *ho'olaule'a*, arts and crafts, food, lei-making. Maui Marriott Resort, Kā'anapali 667-1200

Annual Upcountry Fair—old-fashioned farm fair featuring 4-H farmers' products, a fun run, sports tournaments, entertainment and food booths, and Star Search finals. Eddie Tam Center, Makawao 572-8883

Kapalua Music Festival—internationally acclaimed artists from all over the world assemble to perform chamber music at Kapalua Bay Hotel. Kapalua Music Assembly 669-5273

June–July

Outrigger Canoe Racing—Maui clubs compete for county titles - June through July. Good local food and fun. Check local papers for location.

JULY

Maui Biathlon—5-kilometer run and 800-meter swim in which mostly Maui residents participate. Wailea Beach Park 877-5827

Makawao Statewide Rodeo—popular old-time Upcountry rodeo at Oskie Rice Arena. Annual Makawao 4th of July Rodeo Parade precedes the three-day event. 572-8102

Annual Maui Jaycees Carnival—games, rides, entertainment, food and commercial booths and opening day parade. Kahului Fairgrounds 877-3432

Sauza Cup Races—sponsored by the Lahaina Yacht Club. Scheduled to coincide with the finish of the Transpac and Victoria-to-Maui yacht races. Lahaina 661-0191

Kapalua Wine Symposium—a gathering of wine and food experts for a series of formal tastings, panel discussions and other celebrations of the vine. Pre-registration recommended. Kapalua Bay Hotel 669-0244

Great Kalua Pig Cookoff—competition to select the best pig roasters in the State. Spectators can watch finalists prepare pigs and *imus* [cooking pits] for judging. Royal Lahaina Resort 661-3611 x2291

AUGUST

Haleakala Run to the Sun—an uphill ultramarathon of 36 miles. Finish at top of Haleakalā National Park. Starts at 5:30am at Maui Mall in Kahului. 242-6042

Hawaiian Pro Am—international windsurfing competition featuring three events: Budweiser Slalom Series at Kahana Beach Park; Molokai Channel Crossing from Kapalua to Moloka'i and return; Wailea Speed Crossing from Wailea to Molokini and return. Ehman Productions 579-9765

Plantation Day—cultural demonstrations, entertainment, fashion show, good food, keiki fishing contests. Maui Tropical Plantation (244-7643)

SEPTEMBER

Maui Channel Relay Swim—this 9-mile relay begins on Lāna'i and finishes at Lahaina. 522-7600 (Honolulu)

Kapalua Open Tennis Tournament—top players from around the State compete in this Hawai'i Grand Prix event for one of the largest purses in open and 'B' divisions. Kapalua Tennis Garden 669-0244

Hāna Relay—a 54-mile annual relay run by six-person teams from Kahului to Hāna. Starts at 6am. Valley Isle Road Runners 242-6042

Aloha Week Festivals—Hawaiian pageantry, canoe races, ho'olaule'a, parades, and a variety of entertainment and stage shows. Held on all islands. Aloha Week-O'ahu 944-8857

Cycle to the Sun—38 mile uphill time trial bicycle race. Begins in Paia and climbs to rim of Haleakala. Ehrman Productions 579-9765

Hobie Cat Championships—Kaanapali Beach. Ehrman Productions 579-9765

OCTOBER

Maui County Fair—the State's oldest fair features a grand orchid exhibition, arts and crafts, ethnic foods and a parade to kick off the four-day event. Kahului Fairgrounds 877-5343 or 244-3242

Mazda International Amateur Golf Championships—amateur golfers from around the world gather to compete for $30,000 in prizes. Wailea (879-2966) and Makena (879-3344) Golf Courses

Dracula's Dash— 8 K run. Runners wear Halloween costumes. Begins at Kaanapali Beach 5pm 877-5827

Halloween in Lahaina—Front Street in Lahaina breaks out in Mardi Gras atmosphere with everyone in outrageous costumes.

Halloween Parade—fun for children on Lahaina's Front Street. Benefit for children; community sponsored. October 31, 4pm. 667-7411

October-November

Aloha Classic Wavesailing World Championships—one of the biggest windsurfing contests, with 150 competitors from sixteen countries participating in this ten-day event. $40,000 prize money. Final event of Pro World Tour. Ho'okipa Beach, Pā'ia. Ehman Productions 579-9765

ENTERTAINMENT

109

ENTERTAINMENT

CALENDAR OF EVENTS

NOVEMBER

Na Mele 'O Maui Festival—a festival of Hawaiiana through Hawai'i's arts and crafts, dances, music and a lu'au. Hotels in Kā'anapali and Lahaina. 879-4577

Maui County Rodeo Finals—*paniolo*s [cowboys] from Moloka'i and Maui compete. Top ten contestants take part in finals. Oskie Rice Arena, Makawao 572-9928

Michelob Polo Cup and Bar-B-Cue—an exhibition match of highest rated players from Maui Cup. Olinda Outdoor Polo Field, Makawao. 877-3987

Isuzu Kapalua International Championship Golf—top golf professionals meet at Kapalua Bay Resort for the 'Super Bowl' of golf and one of the sport's largest purses, over $600,000. Spectator admission free. Isuzu Kapalua International 669-4844, 537-1123 (Honolulu)

Thanksgiving Fun Run—Runners estimate completion time for 8.6 or 16.1 mile run. Closest guess wins a turkey. 7am, begins in Rice Park. Kula 242-6042.

DECEMBER

Kapalua/Betsy Nagelsen Tennis Invitational—select field of women professional players, as well as amateurs, in both a pro-doubles competition and pro-am doubles tournament at the Kapalua Bay Resort. Kapalua Tennis Garden 669-5677

The Kirin Cup World Championship of Golf—teams representing the US PGA Tour, the PGA European Tour, the Japan Professional Golf Association Tour and the Australia/New Zealand PGA Tour play the Bay Course, vying for a $900,000 purse. Kirin Cup Tournament Office, Nāpili 669-4844

Santa Comes to Wailea—Santa arrives attired in a red and white lava-lava by way of canoe. Maui Inter-Continental Wailea 879-1922

Wailea Christmas Festival—Wailea Development 879-4465.

Lokahi Pacific Christmas Bazaar—Hawaiian and other homemade Christmas decorations and baked goods for sale. Kahului Shopping Center, Kahului 242-5761

Hui Noeau Christmas House—Christmas arts and crafts of best artists on Maui. Free admission. Hui Noeau Visual Arts Center, Makawao 572-6560

Bodhi Day—Buddhist temples commemorate 'Day of Enlightenment'. All islands. Hawaii Buddhist Council 538-3805 (Honolulu). Statue of founder of Hongwanji sect is draped with flower leis. Lahaina Jodo Mission 661-0640

GTE Kaanapali Golf Classic—Kaanapali Senior Classic purse of $300,000. Tour purses total more than $9.5 million. Kā'anapali. 247-6841 (O'ahu)

SHOPPING

Centers
Aloha wear
Handcrafts
Art

SHOPPING

For most, a vacation is not complete without at least the briefest of shopping expeditions. What's available on Maui and how it is presented reaches all ends of the spectrum. Funky boutiques in Pā'ia and Lahaina, upscale resort shops at the Hyatt Regency Maui, **Wailea Shopping Village** and the **Kapalua Shops**, adjacent to the Kapalua Bay Hotel, and the urban shopping centers in the Central Valley give every kind of shopper an option. Addresses and telephone numbers are listed in the APPENDIX.

CENTERS

One of the oldest shopping centers, **The Wharf** is located opposite the Banyan Tree on Front Street in Lahaina. Some fifty shops and stores sprawl among three stories around a courtyard. The complex contains restaurants, apparel stores strong in Polynesian wear and swimwear, and other specialty shops. Parking here is along Front Street, behind Burger King, behind the center itself between Waine'e and Luakini Streets, and on Dickenson Street. Resort buses stop here, as does the bus from the Sugarcane Train terminal.

Also in Lahaina, at the corner of Front Street and Lahainaluna Road, **Lahaina Market Place**'s cobblestone walkways, kiosks, and shaded courtyard filled with people watchers complete the outdoor bazaar setting. **Parrots of Maui** photographs shoppers with colorful parrots. Parking is along its bordering streets, Front and Lahainaluna.

Just down the street from the famous Banyan Tree is the open-air **505 Front Street** complex. Its two levels house restaurants and retail shops, among them some of the better eel skin outlets. Cars park for free either in the basement of the center or in County lots across the street. The **Lahaina Shopping Center** on Front Street draws many residents from the Lahaina area, and

its anchor store is **Nagasako Super Market**. Made up of several two-story buildings, it covers a large area, parking lot included.

Directly across the street, also fronting on the water, is the newly opened **Lahaina Center**, approximately 75 specialty shops, anchored by Hilo Hatties Fashion Center and home of the Hard Rock Cafe, also ABC Stores. The giant complex has been designed in the architectural style of Old Lahaina.

The **Lahaina Cannery Shopping Center** is at 1221 HonoaPi'ilani Highway on the fringe of Lahaina, and built on the site of an old pineapple cannery. The enclosed mall, the only one with air-conditioning on the island, carries out the cannery theme, and its shops and services are so varied they have no motif. Charming restaurants fill the Food Court, and the parking is free.

The **Lahaina Square Shopping Center**, on Waine'e Street across from Lahaina Shopping Center, is a small, wooden complex with free parking and **Foodland** Supermarket as its main tenant. **Mariner's Alley** at 844 Front Street is made up of two levels with a courtyard, and galleries, boutiques, and the popular watering hole Moose McGilly-cuddy's, upstairs.

In Kā'anapali, **Whalers Village** is the major attraction for shopping.

Outdoor, split in two levels and centered around a marvelous whaling museum, it is known for its different types of art galleries, high end specialty and clothing shops, and dependable restaurants. Mentioned below, **Ka Honu Gift Gallery** and **Sea & Shell Gallery** are two of the shops unique to this center. Parking rates are reasonable at the adjacent lot, and free entertainment in the amphitheater takes place several days of the week.

Located in Kahana on Lower HonoaPi'ilani Road, **Gateway Shopping Center** has Whaler's General Store, Food Pantry and many other stores.

In **Kapalua Shops** next to Kapalua Bay Hotel you can find many stores including Accents, Reyn's, and Longhi's.

Kaahumanu Center, one of the Central Valley shopping centers on Ka'ahumanu Avenue, has more than sixty stores with Hawai'i's own **Liberty House** and Mainland giant **Sears** as its major retail establishments. The center's other shops sell the works. Eateries includes **Ma-Chan's**, and a Japanese department store, **Shirokiya** has the residents' choice, a *bento* (lunch box) at lunchtime.

Just down Ka'ahumanu Avenue from Kaahumanu Center is the **Kahului Shopping Center**, built in the late 1940s and Maui's first shopping center. **Noda's Market** and **Ah Fook's Super Market** are old-time operations that the other shops center around.

The closeby **Maui Mall Shopping Center**, on the same side of the street, underwent major renovation in 1988 and continues to add new specialty shops to its beautifully landscaped complex. The funky **Sir Wilfred's Coffee Tea Tobacco Shop** deserves a look in, along with **JR's Music Shop**, the largest on Maui, and the famous natural food store, **Tasaka Guri Guri Shop** (which makes special local ice cream concoctions using a secret formula). All the staples, **Star Market, Longs Drugs** and **Waldenbooks** can also be found in the Mall. Maui entertainers frequently perform here.

Kukui Mall at 1819 S. Kīhei Rd. has a variety of specialty shops, among them are **Waldenbooks** and **Local Motion Inc.** There is also a coin operated laundry. Lots of free Mall parking.

Closeby on the same street is **Kīhei Town Center**, anchored by **Foodland**. You can find **Chuck's Steak House**, McDonald's, a bank and other stores here.

Azeka Place at 1280 S Kīhei Road in Kīhei began as **Azeka's Market** about thirty years ago and has become a Kīhei staple, servicing the locals with more than forty shops in addition to ample parking. Stores include **Liberty House, O'Rourke's Tourist Trap** and **Wow! Swimwear**, mentioned below.

Kīhei's newest center, located between Kama'ole Beach Park I and II on S Kīhei Road with free parking is the **Kamaole Shopping Center**. Also in Kīhei, opposite Kama'ole Beach Park, is the **Rainbow Mall**, with its mixture of restaurants, clothing and specialty shops, among other businesses.

In Upcountry Maui, the **Pukalani Terrace Center** is easy to find alongside Haleakalā Highway (Route 37). **Foodland, Pukalani Drugs**, banks, and a launderette accommodate the community's needs. A western theme throughout befits the center that Upcountry residents and visitors en route to Haleakalā frequent.

DEPARTMENT STORES

Two home-grown department stores complete with souvenir and aloha wear displays, **Liberty House** and **Ikeda's**, are joined by their Mainland counterparts, **Sears, Ben Franklin, Woolworth** and **National Dollar Stores. Shirokiya**, a Japanese-owned store in Kaahumanu Center, sells many items made in Japan.

ALOHA WEAR

Island clothing cut loose and easy, and the comfortable aloha shirts for men and *mu'umu'us* [long, loose dresses] for women can be found in almost every fabric and weave, usually in bright, flowery prints.

Such fashion is acceptable almost everywhere in the islands; only a scattering of restaurants still demand that men wear jackets. Even so, some men wear aloha shirts under their jackets and enjoy the contrast. The matching aloha shirt-*mu'umu'u* combinations mostly are worn by our cheerful visitors.

Many boutiques, resort shops and department stores merchandise aloha wear. **Liberty House** has a fine selection, as does **Hilo Hattie's**, which shuttles you free from the Lahaina/Kā'anapali area to its fashion center at 1000 Limahana Place, Lahaina. **Muumuu Factory to You** carries aloha wear for the whole family and can be found in the Lahaina Shopping Center. Also geared for children as well as adults, **Leilani Gift Shop** has gift items in addition to island clothing.

More than a dozen shops with aloha wear are located at The Wharf in Lahaina (see Centers above). The well-known local designers include **Tori Richards, Reyn's, Cooke Street, Hawaiian Holidays, Princess Kaiulani Fashions** and **Waltah Clarke**.

T-SHIRTS

The undisputed king of trendy tees in Hawai'i is **Crazy Shirts**, with locations in Lahaina, Kā'anapali and Kīhei. They feature hundreds of original designs, and their Front Street location is home to the owner's private collection of whaling artifacts. The highly visible **T-Shirt Factory** has a wide selction of low-priced tees. **Totally Maui Funwear** has T-shirts and more—all sporty warm weather clothing.

WOMEN'S BOUTIQUES

The emphasis at **Silks Ka'anapali, Ltd.**, in Whalers Village is on originality. Local artists design the images that are painted onto silks, rayons and cotton. Each piece is done individually, with meticulous attention to the marriage of design and fabric. Also located in Whalers Village, the trendy worldwide **Benetton** chain doesn't confine their clothing to one sex.

Judges' Beyond the Reef in Kīhei and **Arabesque** in Lahaina are two other fine shops selling everything from evening and party clothes to stylish work clothes. **Apparels of Pauline** at Lahaina Market Place carries a line of hand-painted clothing by artists from Maui, O'ahu and the island of Hawai'i. Also available are handicrafts, jewelry and accessories from Bali and Asia.

Fashions at **Su-Su's Boutique** in Wailea are young at heart. The store also carries a superb collection of high-quality aloha and resort wear.

Another well known boutique is the **Maui Clothing Company Inc.** in Azeka Place and Lahaina Shopping Center.

At the Kapalua Shops, an elegant and spacious setting for clothes shopping is **Longhi The Shop**; their evening wear selection is one of the best on the island, and they have quality men's fashions as well. Also in the Kapalua Shops, **Mandalay** specializes in custom-designed imports in Thai or antique Japanese silks.

Boutique in Pā'ia to stop in is **The Clothes Addict**, geared for modern dressers. **Tiger Lily** in Kahului is an outstanding boutique that offers clothing by major designers as well as the handiwork of local designers and craftsmen.

Jaggers in Paia on the Hana Highway is a good spot for women's and men's clothing.

MEN'S SHOPS

Men—and women buying gifts for them on Maui—tend to gravitate to **Reyn's** in the Kapalua Shops and at the Lahaina Cannery Center. Reyn's produces the cloth and clothing known as Reyn Spooner, a comfortable and wrinkle-resisting fabric that makes great aloha and resort wear. **Kramer's**, a youth-oriented men's store in Lahaina and Kahului, is where you will find up-to-date fashions, along with **Kula Bay** in Lahaina; their shirts and pants are made of cotton only, and designs that mirror the prints of the forties and fifties are produced here, then manufactured on the Mainland. The shop carries hats, belts, shoes and other apparel, but it is the distinctive local design that has made the store a success.

Fine resort apparel and accessories for men and women can be found at **Andrade** at the Kapalua Shops and other locations, along with the **Kapalua Shop** itself, carrying men's and women's casual resort sportswear and stylish gifts.

Kula Bay on Lahainaluna off Front Street in Lahaina offers a unique selection of high quality men's tropical wear.

HANDCRAFTS

Maui on My Mind, located in Whaler's Village and Lahaina Cannery, sells gift items of traditional Hawaiian heritage—handcrafted koa, *lauhala* and fiber baskets, Hawaiian quilts and coral and abalone jewelry. **Ka Honu Gift Gallery** has one-of-a-kind handmade gift items and a Christmas ornament section that is stocked year-round with originals made by local artisans.

Maui's Best in Kā'anapali, Kahului, and Wailea sells arts and crafts created by local artists, in addition to clothing, books, wood-carvings, prints, foodstuffs, jewelry and other items. Another store with exclusive gift items—water color originals, pottery, and brass figurines—is **Elephant Walk**, with outlets in Ka'anapali hotels, Wailea Village and on Front St. in Lahaina.

Visitors will find crafts made with 'native' or natural materials by local artists at the **Maui Crafts' Guild**.

LEATHER GOODS

Leather goods—belts, purses, and briefcases—can be found at **Maui Moorea Leather & Gifts** in Makawao and at **Lahaina Shoe & Luggage Repair**, specializing in custom-made belts and sandals.

Residents and visitors of Maui shop around for eelskin purses, wallets, belts, bags and other products, as the prices here are among the lowest in the nation.

A good portion of Market Street, in the heart of Wailuku, is devoted to eelskin shops. In Lahaina the eelskin outlets are: **Front Street Wholesale Eelskin** and **Eelskin Factory Outlet** (also in Wailuku), and **Golden Eel Import Company**. Located in Kīhei, **Lady Di's**, although it carries everything from Black Hills gold to greeting cards, is known for its selection of eelskin products.

JEWELRY

Jewelry manufacturers and stores in the Islands do not limit themselves to but specialize in treasures from the sea and shore, and many custom design. At the **Lahaina General Store** you can find a local tradition—leis, bracelets and earrings made from the rare, tiny shells painstakingly gathered from the beaches of the privately owned island of Ni'ihau. This shell stands alone as the only kind that is classified as a gem and that can be insured. Another tradition, Hawaiian 'heirloom' jewelry, generally takes longer than a brief visit to have custom made; bracelets, pendants and rings are made of heavy gold bearing the wearer's name approximated in Hawaiian and enameled in black Victorian lettering. **Maui Wholesale Gold** sells such jewelry plus many styles of chains and charms. **Kaneshige Jewelers**, a store dating back to 1894, also stocks Hawaiian heirloom jewelry, in addition to diamonds,

jade and other fine gemstones. One more to try is **Emura Jewelers** in Wailuku for Hawaiian jewelry and low-priced eelskin. Ivory, scrimshaw, and Oriental carvings make **Lahaina Scrimshaw** much more than just a jewelry store.

Antique netsuke—the closures on purses that were slipped over the sash of the kimono in old Japan—are rare, expensive, and available through only seven dealers in the world. However, contemporary souvenir netsuke, made in Hong Kong or Japan for the tourist trade, can be found at many gift shops around Maui.

Claire, the Ring Lady in Lahaina will design creations in gold, silver and other precious metals while you wait. Exotic black pearls from Tahiti are also popular in custom designing one-of-a-kind pieces.

Daring divers going to greater and greater depths in the waters off Maui bring up gold, pink and black coral stems, which are then highly polished and designed into unique pieces of jewelry. Founded by Jack Ackerman, who rediscovered coral after its 400-year disappearance, **Jack Ackerman's The Original Maui Divers** on Front Street has an extensive collection of coral, Ni'ihau shells, and pearls.

The **Coral Grotto**, located at the Pioneer Inn, Sheraton-Maui, Kihei Town Center, and many other jewelry stores showcase these unusual and beautiful pieces of coral. The ubiquitous **Pearl Factory**, selling out of shops and kiosks, ends the search for the pearl in the oyster.

ART

Maui has slowly become one of the major centers of art in Hawai'i. Many artists live here either part time or year-round, and more and more are achieving international recognition while showing a fierce loyalty to the Islands. In their wake, the island has attracted major art exhibits. The annual Art Maui event is a splendid celebration of both well-known artists and talented newcomers (see CALENDAR OF EVENTS).

The list begins with internationally recognized Maui resident **Robert Lyn Nelson** and his paintings of two worlds—above and below the surface of the sea. Paris-born **Guy Buffet**, an impressionistic artist in a primitive setting, has had an ongoing love affair with Hawai'i that keeps him living and working on Maui, and selling internationally. Watercolorist and world peace artist **Andrea Smith** recently was honored by the United Nations for her works. Residing on O'ahu, the **Makk Family**, originally from Hungary, exhibits their impressionist paintings in the traditional European style exclusively—as does Buffet and Smith—at the **Lahaina Galleries**.

Jan Kasprzycki, a transplanted Californian who lives in Upcountry, is a master oil-painter and works in powerful contrasts of colors and light. The list continues: **Hisashi Otsuka** does spectacular work based on classical Japanese art; **Lau Chun's** impressionist paintings are a mainstay of the Maui scene; China-born **H. Leung**, also lives and paints on Maui; **Gary Swanson**, a foremost wildlife painter, portrays cats from all over the world; and **George Allan**, **Chris Lassen**, and **Andrew Annenberg's** works are hung in prized collections around the world.

Pegge Hopper, well-known for her colorful large Hawaiian women, exhibits on Maui. **Margaret Keane's** wide-eyed children can be found at many shops. Actor **Anthony Quinn** and comedian **Red Skelton** exhibit their originals at the Mainland chain of **Center Art Galleries**.

R.C. Gorman, who represents the vigor and inventivness of the Taos painters, is represented by the **Sunset Gallery** with two locations in Lahaina.

There are as many galleries as artists in this hub of the island art scene. Lahaina Galleries Inc., one of the oldest, has several locations, including **Lahaina Gallery** on Front Street, Lahainaluna Road, and at The Wharf; **Gallery Ka'anapali** in Whalers Village; and **Kapalua Gallery** in Kapalua. The **Village Gallery** and **The Village Gallery-Lahaina**, both in Lahaina, have Hawaiiana and Mainland art. The **Dyansen Gallery of Maui**, part of a Mainland chain and located in Whaler's Village and on Front Street, contains displays of widely acclaimed art, objets d'art, sculptures of Erte and rare sketches of the late John Lennon.

The small **Curtis Wilson Cost Gallery** in the Kula Lodge handles only the artist's own works, while the **Larry Dotson Gallery & Studio** in Lahaina also features the owner's sculpture and seascapes. **Dolphin Galleries** in the Lahaina Cannery Center and several other locations is considered a craft gallery with posters and some sculpture. The **Coast Gallery** at the Intercontinental in Wailea handles original art by local artists.

Often a starting point for young artists, the **Old Jail Gallery** on Wharf Street is located at the site of a historic jail, near the Banyan Tree in the heart of Lahaina.

Provenance Gallery at Lahaina Market Place exhibits world class art—oils, graphics and objets d'art— of the old masters and contemporaries such as Guillaume Azoulay, Robert Blue and Eyvind Earle.

SOUVENIRS

In addition to hotel shops and department stores, many Hawaiian gift and souvenir items can be found at the ubiquitous **ABC Discount Stores.** They have eight locations on Maui: five in Lahaina, one each in Honokōwai, Kā'anapali and Kīhei. **A to Z Stores** have what their name implies and four locations: three in Lahaina and one in Nāpili. In Kīhei Town Center, **Hawaiian Etc** also carry the souvenirs you'll want to take home for gifts. On Market Street in Old Wailuku Town is **'Antique Row'** with shops of a cultural nature selling many one of a kind items. **Island Camera & Gift Shops** stock souvenirs in addition to photographic products, and can be found in a few hotels as well as at Wailea Village. **Longs Drug Stores,** in Lahaina and Kahului, sell the same variety of products, along with **Woolworth** in the Maui Mall in Kahului. **Hawaiian Experience Omni Theatre** features a 40 minutes film on the hour, every hour, about the experience of Hawaii. It has a gift shop in the theatre, plus a sister shop at the Lahaina Train Depot.

Other souvenir shops are: **EZ Discount Store, Paradise Lahaina,** and **Whaler's General Stores** in Lahaina; EZ Discount Store has numerous locations in Lahaina, Nāpili and Kīhei. Also the various hotel lobby shops—**Leisure Sundries,** Maui Prince Hotel; **Traders** and **Whaler's Chest,** Royal Lahaina Resort; **South Pacific Gifts & Sundries,** Westin Maui; **WH Smith,** Stouffer Wailea Beach Resort; **Accents,** Maui Inter-Continental Wailea and Hyatt Grand in Wailea; **Lamont's,** Hyatt Regency Maui, Four Seasons Resort Wailea, Embassy Suites in Lahaina; and the **Lobby Shop,** Maui Marriott Resort.

Another one-stop gift shop with hundreds of knickknacks to choose from, including Hummel figurines, is **O'Rourke's Tourist Trap,** with two locations and open 365 days a year. **Accents** at the Kapalua Shops is a cross between a drugstore, a newsstand and a gift shop.

SHELLS

Many visitors like to take home shells from their island vacation, but few are found on Maui's accessible beaches. **Sea & Shell Gallery**, which has several outlets, features rare and unusual shells, corals, woods from Bali, jewelry and sculptures for the collector. **The Shell Stop!** near mile marker 18 along Hāna Highway and **Jane's Shells & Craft**, in Pā'ia, are other alternatives.

FRUITS, FLOWERS and FOLIAGE

One of Maui's prized flowers is the protea, transplanted from Australia and South Africa and exotic in its many different shapes and colors. At the **Upcountry Protea Farm** in Kula visitors can enjoy a free walk through the gardens displaying the ten- to twenty-foot plants. The Farm can arrange the shipping of plants and blossoms. In the Wailuku area, the **Plantation Marketplace** in Maui Tropical Plantation sells many unique gift items, most of which are edible: pineapples, papayas, macadamia nuts, and a unique blend of Maui coffee.

Many visitors want to take home fresh Hawaiian fruits, flower leis, cuttings and seeds, or colorful tropical plants. This is easy to arrange; many vendors will ship purchases for you. Some fruits and flowers are subject to quarantine regulations imposed by the US Department of Agriculture and are prohibited from entry to Mainland states. Pineapples and coconuts are no problem, but the only papayas allowed are those that have been inspected. **Airport Flower & Fruit**, three minutes from Kahului Airport and in Lahaina, sells fruit that have been treated and passed by agricul-

A friendly artist selling her T-shirts, roadside at Wailua Falls.

tural inspectors. They will deliver them to the Airport with pre-payment. **A-1 Pineapples** handles free airport deliveries of this fruit in addition to Maui onions and protea.

Be cautious when buying leis to take home. Flowers such as roses, *maunaloa* and jade, mock orange and *mokihana* berries, and leaves such as *hala* and *kikuyu* are prohibited, and leis containing them will be confiscated.

Sterile cuttings and seeds of many tropical and semitropical plants are sold in sealed packages that have been passed and certified by the US Department of Agricul-ture, and these will pass inspection without difficulty. They are sold in many souvenir shops and in almost all plant and garden shops.

West Maui Florist & Nursery is the only florist at the south end of Lahaina, and they have years of experience in packing and mailing tropical flowers as well as being qualified floral consultants for special parties and weddings. **Lahaina Florist** and **Take Home Maui** are other dependable shops for arranging the shipping of flowers; they're located in the Lahaina Shopping Center.

BOOKS

Waldenbooks, the national chain, has five stores in Maui: two outlets in Kahului, one each in Kīhei, Lahaina and Kā'anapali. All stores carry a good variety of calendars, magazines, videocassettes, newspapers and other paper products in addition to books.

Miracles Unlimited and Herbs, **Etc.** in Wailuku offer a variety of new age books.

The **Silversword Book and Card Store** in Azeka Place has children's books, cards, stationery and a few gift items. The **Whaler's Book Shoppe & Coffee House** at The Wharf has a substantial Hawaiiana selection.

GROCERIES

Visitors whose accommodations include cooking facilities may wish to take a break from dining out and prepare a home-cooked meal. Local supermarkets carry all the items you are used to, and a lot more, including many Asian foods. Grocery stories include: **Foodland**, at Kaahumanu Center, Lahaina Square Center, Pukalani Terrace Shopping Center, and Kīhei Town center; **Safeway** opens 24 hours, has one store each in Lahaina and Kahului; **Star Markets**, in Kahului and Kīhei; **Hāna Ranch Store** in Hāna; and **Azeka's Market** at Azeka Place. **Nagasako's Super Market** in Lahaina offers a variety of local foods. Located in Wailea Village, **Wailea Pantry** carries gift and beach items in addition to food and beverages. If you're staying on the North Shore, the **Honokowai Food Pantry** services the area.

CONVENIENCE STORES

Operating twenty-four hours a day, the two **7-Eleven Food Stores** on the island are located in Kīhei and Kahului. Keeping the same hours are **Circle K** in Lahaina and **The Minit Stop** in Wailuku, Kahului and Pukalani.

In Lahaina, **Handi Pantry** has one outlet. **Whalers General Store** has numerous locations in Lahaina and Kīhei. **Wailea Pantry** operates out of Wailea Village.

HEALTH FOOD STORES

A local institution is the **Paradise Fruit Stand** in Kīhei (across from McDonald's on Kīhei Road). This produce stand/restaurant also packs fruit for shipping. **Down to Earth** in Wailuku and **Westside Natural Foods** in Lahaina sell natural foods and products including cream, lotion, and shampoo made from pure kukui nut oil. In Wailuku, **Herbs Etc** has a complete line of herbs, teas and vitamins. **Mana Foods** services Pā'ia residents, and **Mountain Fresh Market**, Upcountry folks. Two smaller stores, **Maui Natural Foods** is located in the Maui Mall Center, and **The Health Spot** is in Kīhei's Kukui Mall.

DRUGSTORES

There are enough on Maui to meet the needs of residents and visitors. By area, they include: Lahaina, **Longs Drug Store,** Lahaina Cannery Center; Kīhei, **Kīhei Drug,** 1881 S Kīhei Road; Upcountry, **Pukalani Drugs,** inside the Foodland Store of Pukalani Terrace Center; and Central Valley, **Valley Isle Pharmacy,** 2180 Main Street, **Pay 'n Save,** 200 E Kamehameha Avenue, **Toda Drugs,** Kahului Center, and **Longs Drug Store** in the Maui Mall. Besides these, there are many other pharmacies throughout the island.

MISCELLANEOUS

For photographic equipment and film processing, **Wailea 1 Hour Photo** in Wailea Village is a high quality shop. **Fox Photo** also has one-hour processing and has five locations in West Maui as well as in Kīhei and Wailea.

Mark's Hallmark Shop in Kaahumanu Center carries little gifts and cards. **Hopaco Stationers** also has a selection of cards, and is known for their office supplies.

One of the many colorful and exotic variations of protea.

Fine dining
Fun dining
Special foods
Shave ice

FINE and FUN DINING

Maui's restaurants fit any taste, budget and mood. From lavishly prepared French cuisine to exotic Asian dishes, the eating establishments on Maui are as fine as you will find in any resort area. From Kā'anapali settings with spectacular sunset views to the fireplaces of cozy lounges in Upcountry, it is the variety in Maui restaurants, like the variety of Maui itself, that makes dining here a joy.

FINE DINING

In this chapter, we have divided Maui into regions and then provided a sampling of restaurants in each area. While our list of dining options features a great deal of variety, the establishments share the one common characteristic of good restaurants—the food is good enough to keep you coming back. Given that, the style, decor, service and ambience may differ greatly, but all add to your dining experience. The criteria we used in our selection of restaurants are as follows:

- physical property
- decor and lighting
- china and napery
- ambience
- quality of appropriate wine list
- service
- price in relation to food
- melding of menu items
- texture and taste of food
- a memorable essence of greatness

The prices indicated here are per person and do not include drinks. Most fine dining establishments accept major credit cards. The following symbols are used to help you in your choices:

B	Breakfast
L	Lunch
D	Dinner
R	Reservations suggested
J	Jacket required
E	Entertainment/dancing
W	Wheelchair access
$$$$	$40 +
$$$	$30-$40
$$	$15-$30
$	$10-$15

On Maui, where fresh seafood is served frequently, prices vary greatly according to the day's catch. Also, prices indicated here are dinner prices; restaurants and dining rooms that also serve lunch almost always have less expensive prices on their luncheon menu.

LAHAINA/KĀʻANAPALI

Gerard's ★★★★★ $$$/$$$$ R / D

Like dining in a French country inn, with enchanting ambience, delicious sauces in addition to appetizers that change daily and a superior wine list. Owner/chef Gerard Reversade is from France's Armagnac region. 174 Lahainaluna Road, Lahaina 661-8939

Sound of the Falls ★★★★★ $$/$$$$ B L D

French elegance and Pacific romance, high-ceiling open room with a view of the falls as well as sound and surrounded by lagoons with graceful swans and coral flamingos sailing by lagoon-side tables. Breakfast is buffet or served, delicious either way; lunch is buffet and dinner is superb. For appetizers, broiled Hawaiian baby abalone with *porcini* in chive sauce; for entree, medallions of veal with ragout of *shiitake* and sweetbreads, two of 27 menu items. Complimentary hors d'oeuvres begin each meal, complimentary chocolates end it. The Westin Maui, Kāʻanapali 667-2525

Swan Court ★★★★★ $$$/$$$$ B D

Elegant, award-winning dining alongside a pool graced by live swans. Varied and imaginative menu; sophisticated simplicity and first-class operation. Outstanding wine selection. Hyatt Regency Kāʻanapali 667-7474

Chez Paul ★★★★ $$$/$$$$ R / D

Tucked away in Olowalu, this was an "insider's" secret for years. Intimate restaurant with impeccable service and a concentration on fine French cuisine. Menu changes constantly, but is consistently delicious. Chez Paul is the only restaurant, not located in a hotel, to receive the Holiday Travel Award on Maui, for two years in a row. Excellent wine list. Reservations are essential. 820-B Olowalu Village 661-3843

David Paul's Lahaina Grill ★★★★ $$$/$$$$ R / L D

This intimate restaurant on Lahainaluna Road has a menu full of delectable dishes with southwestern spice added just for fun. The Tequilla Shrimp is the signature dish, but any of the appetizers or entrees are exciting. Chocolate-lovers will revel in the flavor of the chocolate pate. Turn of the century decor and a intimate bar create an airy cafe atmosphere. 127 Lahainaluna Road 667-5117

La Bretagne ★★★ $$/$$$ L D

Fine dining in a French home atmosphere, with intimate tables, outstanding service and a blend of the best of French country cooking and fresh island foods. French house wines; unforgettable desserts. 562-C Front Street, off Shaw Street, around the corner, Lahaina 661-8966

LAHAINA/KĀ'ANAPALI

Longhi's ★★★ $$/$$$ E / B L D

Big, busy with a justly deserved reputation as a Maui favorite. Pasta made on the spot, fresh seafood and a range of desserts; lively atmosphere. Upstairs is a traditional dining room; downstairs, a bistro-like area open to the sidewalk and the sea beyond. No menu and no posted daily specials. Waiters recite the extensive repertoire of items.   888 Front Street, Lahaina 667-2288

Mango Jones ★★★ $$$ R / D

Overlooking Kā'anapali Resort, Mango Jones offers sundown specials from 5:30 pm to 6:30pm and Karaoke singing on Thursday, Friday and Saturday. Kā'anapali Resort 667-6847

Nikko Steakhouse ★★★ $$ R / D

Opulent Eastern pleasure-dome setting featuring a harmony of good Asian foods, prepared by chefs who know both their food and their *teppan* showmanship. Spicy, succulent dishes. Maui Marriott Hotel, Kā'anapali 667-1200

Maui Rose ★★★ $$$ R / D

Glorious ocean views, Hawaiian seafood and much more are the featured attractions of this restaurant which opens at 5:30pm and offers nightly entertainment. Embassy Suites 661-2000

KAPALUA

The Plantation Veranda ★★★★★ $$$ R J / D

An inviting "plantation home" with glass doors opening into a courtyard garden and striking Pegge Hopper murals. The menu includes such favorites as duck, liver mousse flavored with plum wine, medallions of lobster, and escalopes of spring lamb. The wine list has been named the top 100 in the U.S. Consummate Cookery. Kapalua Resort 669-5656

Garden Restaurant ★★★★★ $$$ B D

Fine al fresco dining accompanied by meandering streams and panoramic views of the Pacific ocean are offered in this garden restaurant featuring wonderfully-prepared regional, American and continental cuisine at breakfast and dinner. Excellent wine list and service. Cocktails also served. A Mayfair Buffet is served on Sundays. Kapalua Resort 669-0244

The Bay Club ★★★ $$/$$$ R J / L D

A popular tropical restaurant atop the promontory fronting Kapalua Bay, The Bay Club offers a a great view and lively atmosphere. Lunch, dinner and cocktails served daily featuring a luncheon salad bar, fine wine list, and live entertainment. Kapalua Resort 669-5656

Pineapple Hill ★★★★ $$/$$$ R / D

Fine dining in an old plantation house, with artifacts and antiques of that era. Good sunset view, perfect vistas of Moloka'i and Lāna'i. Continental menu; best pineapple daiquiris. Above Kapalua Bay Resort 669-6129

Sea House Restaurant ★★ $/$$ R / B L D

An old Maui landmark with a new menu and name (formerly the Teahouse of the Maui Moon). Relaxed, seaside setting. Try the macadamia nut chicken with a sweet sour sauce. Napili Kai Beach Club, 5900 HonoaPi'ilani Hwy, Nāpili 669-6271

KĪHEI/WAILEA/MĀKENA

La Perouse ★★★★★ $$/$$$ R J E / D

Award-winning restaurant, decorated with Oriental silks and African antiques, features French cuisine with touches of Hawai'i. Seafood is the specialty, but beef, veal, lamb and duck are outstanding as well. Wine selection ranks in the top 100, according to *The Wine Spectator*. Maui Inter-Continental Wailea 879-1922

Prince Court ★★★★★ $$/$$$ R / D

One of Maui's more polished restaurants. Well-prepared American food; Hawaiian prawns, lobster and scallops; lavish desserts such as macadamia nut brittle flan. Sunday brunch is probably the best on the island. Maui Prince Hotel, Mākena 874-1111

Raffles ★★★★★ $$/$$$ J / D

Elegant Asian theme, fine menu and excellent service; award-winning continental cuisine served in a sophisticated setting. Named after the Raffles Hotel in Singapore, an Asian landmark and one of the best hotels in the Orient. Elegant Sunday brunch. Stouffer Wailea Beach Resort 879-4900

Kihei Prime Rib & Seafood ★★★ $$$ D

Oceanfront dining in the heart of Kihei. Fresh fish, prime rib and gourmet salad bar featured. 2511 S. Kīhei Road 879-1954

Hakone ★★★ $$ R / D

An elegantly managed restaurant with a touch of old Japan, authentic Japanese cuisine and decor, and a sushi bar. Efficient service and attention to detail. Sounds of a Japanese koto linger in the air. Maui Prince Hotel, Mākena 874-1111

PĀ'IA/UPCOUNTRY

Mama's Fish House ★★★ $$/$$$ R W / L D

South Seas oceanside restaurant on a beautiful beach where there is windsurfing and an occasional whale sighting. Decor features mementos from French Polynesia, plus gifts from the sea—shells, floats, fishing nets, nautical gear. Chef has well-earned reputation for fresh seafood dishes. Just past Pā'ia, in Kū'au, 799 Kaiholo Place 579-9672

Makawao Steak & Fish House ★★★ $/$$ R / D

Pleasant ambience and a nice lounge showcasing Hawai'i's artists, plus a fire in the fireplace on cool nights. An excellent salad bar and a variety of entrees. Try mud pie for dessert. 3612 Baldwin Avenue, Makawao 572-8711

Casanova Italian Deli ★★★ $ B L D

Some of the finest Italian pastas anywhere. To eat here, take-out or to cook. Taste treats include eggplant parmesan, *gnocchi*, 'homemade' pastas, cannelloni with crab, espresso, cappuccino, pastries and cannoli. Noodles, angel hair and linguini in wonderful colors and flavors—tomato, basil, wild mushroom, lemon, anchovy, red pepper, black pepper and spinach. New, large fine dining room. 1188 Makawao Avenue (Four Corners) 572-0220

Kula Lodge ★★ $/$$ R / B L D

Upcountry oasis and a favorite among residents, this restaurant features a lounge fireplace and picture windows affording magnificent views of West Maui. Lunchtime favorites are Portuguese bean soup and *mahimahi*; spicy shrimp curry for dinner. Haleakalā Highway 878-1535

HĀNA

Hotel Hāna-Maui ★★★★★ $$$/$$$$ R E / B L D

This hotel dining room has the many charms of a slow-paced, earlier Hawaiian era. Newly rebuilt, the large, gracious room features beautiful local woods, views of Hāna Bay and myriad tropical blossoms. American-Pacific cuisine with a touch of southern US and southern France cookery; fresh Hawaiian beef, seafood, chicken and vegetables take on wonderful flavors. Attentive service, excellent wine list. Hotel Hāna-Maui 248-8211

WAILUKU-KAHULUI

The Chart House ★★★ $$ R / D

Nautical theme and ocean view provide a chance to see cruise ships depart.

Simple food. Fresh fish, tasty teriyaki steak, or a combination of meat and seafood; outstanding salad bar. Good, dependable service. Reservations strongly recommended. 500 N Pu'unēnē Avenue, Kahului 877-2476

Ming Yuen ★★★ $ R W / L D

Off the beaten path, but worth seeking out, this 'Illustrious Courtyard' offers Cantonese and Szechwan cooking with seafood specialties. Good service and pleasing decor featuring authentic Chinese antiques that make this a showplace setting. 162 Alamaha Street, Kahului 871-7787

Siam Thai ★★ $ L D

A taste of Thailand in an unpretentious but pleasant setting; ceiling fans give the feel of Asia. Vegetables and spices grown on Maui by the owners' family. Favorites include coconut-chicken soup and *satay*—beef, pork, chicken or tofu—prepared in a spicy peanut sauce. Some Chinese dishes. 123 N Market Street, Wailuku 244-3817

FUN DINING

Maui also offers dining options that may not fit into the Fine Dining category above, but do provide the visitor with a variety of taste treats as well as just plain fun.

Our informal listing below separates these restaurants into regions. For more information about a Hawaiian lu'au, see ENTERTAINMENT.

LAHAINA/KĀ'ANAPALI

Alex's Hole in the Wall $$ R / L D

A small family restaurant that features homemade pastas, sausages, and cheese cake. Open for lunch and dinner. Full bar and select wine list. 834 Front Street, down Wahiee Lane 661-3197

Avalon Restaurant & Bar $$ L D

Shaded courtyard dining in Lahaina's Mariner's Alley, features Hawaiian/Asian/California dishes. Chinese chicken salad, steamed New Zealand clams, wok-sauteed plantains (cooking bananas) and guacamole made fresh table-side. Mariner's Alley, Lahaina 667-5559

Bettino's Restaurant & Lounge $ B L D

Beautiful ocean views served with early morning breakfasts, and sunsets with dinner. Seafood is featured, and the shrimp scampi is particularly good along with the seafood salads. 505 Front Street, Lahaina 661-8810

Chopsticks $$ R E / L D

The first restaurant on Maui to offer 'grazing', a new concept in vacation dining

DINING

of serving many special food items in appetizer portions. Diners may select one or many dishes a la carte of selections from the Pacific and Asia. Royal Lahaina Resort 661-3611

China Boat $$/$$$ R/LD

In Kahana near the West Maui Airport, this lovely restaurant offers fine cuisine prepared in the old Chinese style, featuring a wide range of seafood and meats. Karaoke singing on Friday and Saturday. 4474 Lower HonoaPiʻilani Rd. 669-5089

Cook's at the Beach $$ BLD

A plethora of tasty choices for any time of day with a view of Westin Maui's waterworld, and attentive service. Breakfast omelets, *fritattas*, benedicts; salads and sandwiches; appetizers and soups both hot and cold or dinner entrees from Southern fried chicken to steamed Oriental vegetables, yummy desserts. The Westin Maui, Kāʻanapali 667-2525

Denny's $ BLD

So good they received a special mention from Robert Balzer. Inexpensive, bountiful breakfasts, good prices, good food. The menus feature 138 different items—around the clock in Lahaina, 'til midnight in Kīhei. Lahaina Square Shopping Center 667-7898; Kamaole Shopping Center, Kīhei 879-0604

El Crab Catcher $$ E/LD

Marvelous oceanfront location on Kāʻanapali Beach, number one place for girl watching, also whale watching and other beautiful views. Features fresh local fish, steaks and prime ribs. Noted for beer-steamed crab legs and Hula Pie. Poolside *pūpū*s during the day. Whaler's Village, Kāʻanapali 661-4423

Hard Rock Cafe $$ LD

The latest of this popular chain of restaurants has come to the Lahaina Center and features live rock music as well as a rock'n'roll memorabilia museum and "all-American" style food. Lahaina Center, Front Street, Lahaina 667-7400

Kimo's $$ LD

A favorite of locals and observant visitors. A large downstairs bar hung right over the water, breathtaking at sunset. Lunch and dinner, which run the gamut from huge steakburgers to prime rib, fresh caught fish and steaks are served upstairs in a room of redwood and nautical decor with an even more spectacular view. 845 Front Street, Lahaina 661-4811

Kobe Steak House $$ D

Entire dinners are prepared at cozy *teppan* [grill] tables by the daring young chef's of the flying knives. Teriyaki chicken, hibachi steak, lobster tail and steak, and *teppan* shrimp become deliciously different with the oils and flavorings and the deft grill work. Dinners include *teppan* vegetables, *miso* or mushroom soup, rice, tea and dessert. Show and dinner in one. 136 Dickenson Street (behind Baldwin Home), Lahaina 667-5555

Lahaina Provision Company $$ R / L D

A wonderfully tropical, hidden nooks-and-crannies restaurant. Lunch and dinner, bountiful and exotic buffets. Also excellent a la carte menu, salads, appetizers, fresh fish and US beef. Most famous, and justly so, for the 'Choco-holic's Dessert Bar', pure heaven for diners with a sweet tooth. Hyatt Regency Kā'anapali 661-1234

Leilani's on the Beach $$ D

On the shore at Kā'anapali Beach, a special sunset spot for *pūpūs* and cocktails from 4pm. Dinner specialties are local fish, prime rib and barbequed ribs in a lava rock and koa wood setting. Whalers Village, Kā'anapali 661-4495

Moose McGillycuddy's $ E / B L D

A favorite of locals and visitors and familiar to many who discovered Moose's in college. Neat breakfasts, famous happy hour, bar menu—pizza, hot wings, potato skins, nachos, chicken strips; dinner menu—prime rib, fried chichen, broiled local fish. 844 Front Street, Lahaina 667-7758

Nanatomi Seafood and Steak Restaurant $$ R E / B L D

The great American breakfast starts the day; lunch and dinner present everybody's favorite steaks and a full cast of seafood characters from lobster to scampi and from grilled *'ahi* to poached salmon in eye-appealing presentations, and at reasonable prices. Kā'anapali Pkwy at the entrance to Kaanapali Beach Hotel 667-7902

Pioneer Inn $$ E / B L D

Hawaiian princes, whalers and sailors, opium runners, missionaries and South Seas captains have all dined in the Harbor Room, and drunk their sasparilla and rum grog on the ample porches. A visit to Maui is simply not complete without a meal or cocktails at this bustling inn overlooking the small boat harbor and the Lahaina Roads where in the 1830s more than 200 sailing vessels would be at anchor in one day. The chef prepares a wide variety of island favorites as well as steaks and seafood. Lahaina Harborfront 661-3636

The Rusty Harpoon Restaurant $$ B L D

A prolific menu features Belgian waffles for breakfast, a variety of sandwiches, salads and homemade pasta for lunch, and fresh island fish and prime rib for dinner. Late suppers may be ordered from the Tavern Menu and the colorful view of the action on Ka'anapali Beach and of the Pacific Ocean is available any time. Whalers Village, Kā'anapali Beach 661-3123

Spats $$$ R E / D

The restaurant and disco that has become a legend in its own time. Famous for cozy meals and "Pasta with Passion." The dancing is good fun, the Northern Italian cuisine is good food. Hyatt Regency Maui, Kā'anapali 667-7474 x59

DINING

131

Sam's Beachside Grill $$ L D

The Sunday Brunch (menu style) at this pretty ocean-view restaurant with wide-open doors and potted flowers, is known for Sam's famous Ramos Fizz. An interesting beginning to any week. Concentrating on local fish, the menu also ventures out to rack of lamb, roast duck with papaya, Maui bouillabaisse, chilled artichoke, vegetable fritters, fish and chips and smoked chicken salad. 505 Front Street, Lahaina 667-4341

KĪHEI/WAILEA/MĀKENA

Erik's Seafood Broiler $$ L D

Outstanding display of fresh island fish and outstanding menu presenting local fish, island lobster and prawns, and shell fish from South Pacific waters. Plus halibut and salmon from the cold waters of Alaska and plump catfish from Louisiana. There are steak and lobster combinations and for those who prefer—steaks and chops. A broiler for all reasons. Kamaole Shopping Center, Kīhei 879-8400

Island Thai $$ L D

Fine Thai food mild to hot, cooked to order. Great vegetarian dishes are also offered as well as take-out orders. Azeka's Place, Kīhei 874-0813

Rainbow Lagoon $$$ R / D

Upstairs in Kihei's Rainbow Mall, Rainbow Lagoon specializes in steaks and seafood, with a salad bar. Entertainment nightly except Sundays. Rainbow Mall 879-5600

Sandcastle at Wailea $$ L D

Mesquite broiled fresh fish, succulent steak and chicken are the house specialties in this friendly open-air garden setting. Lunch, earlybird dinner and full dinner are served and *pūpūs* and cocktails fountainside from 4pm. Wailea Shopping Village 879-0606

Set Point $$ B L

Above the Wailea Tennis Club, the Set Point offers light and lively breakfast and lunch menus along with views of the court action and the ocean beyond. Wailea Tennis Club 879-3244

KAPALUA

Erik's Seafood Grotto $$ D

Serves only dinners, but it's all so good most people wish they'd open for lunch. They do offer hot and cold *pūpūs* poolside at sunset. Maui's largest selection of fresh fish is displayed and served here. Following a few libations of Passionate Grog, everything looks as good as it is. Favorites are crab imperial, or coquilles St Jacques and any one of the eleven delicious island fish that may be the catch of the day—also steaks, chicken and lamb. Kahana Villas, Kahana Maui 669-4806

Kapalua Grill & Bar $/$$ L D

A popular restaurant in an informal setting on the golf course at Kapalua. Diverse menu features fresh fish, steaks and chops. Hula Pie is the popular choice for dessert. 200 Kapalua Drive 669-5653

Market Cafe $$ B L D

Like unexpectedly finding a pearl in an oyster, this intimate, informal but classy little cafe is the other half of a store featuring gourmet dining items. Italian cuisine emphasizing freshness and quality. Outstanding service. Kapalua Shops, Kapalua Bay Resort 669-4888

Orient Express $$ D

A delicious potpourri of Thai cuisine with old favorites and new experiences. Everything is prepared to order by the award-winning Thai chef from Bangkok who recommends the Pla Rad Plik and the combination clay pot of fresh fish and seafood, and roasted duck salad. Napili Shores Resort 669-8077

WAILUKU-KAHULUI

Luigi's Pasta & Pizzeria $$ D

Pizza and burgers galore along with Karaoke on Friday and Saturday; disco on Wednesday and Thursday. Maui Mall 877-3761

Mickey's $$ R W / L D

An oasis for local businesspeople as well as visitors, almost hidden from the crowds; pleasing atmosphere, superb salads. Excellent scallops, excellent service. Chocolate Decadence is a dessert favorite. 33 Lono Avenue, Kahului 871-7555

UPCOUNTRY

Fu Wah $$ L D

In the Pukalani Terrace Center, Fu Wah presents family dinner combinations, great Szechuan food, sizzling platters and braised pot courses. Take out also available. Pukalani Terrace Center 572-1341

DINING

133

DINING

UPCOUNTRY

Haliimaile General Store $$$ R / L D

This charming old 1929 general store, in the midst of a 1,000 acre pineapple plantation, has become a favorite gathering spot for world-wide visitors. 572-2666

Pukalani Terrace Country Clubhouse $$ R / L D

Local favorites such as kalua pig, laulau, pulahu ribs offered here along with a large salad bar and varied American menu. Pukalani Golf Course 572-1325

SPECIAL FOODS

Some food found here separates Maui from the rest of the islands. We would be remiss if we didn't take special note of them. One is **Tasaka Guri Guri** in the Maui Mall Shopping Center in Kahului. Guri Guri is a concoction of ice cream and sherbet and possibly something else; we say 'possibly' because the Tasakas won't tell anybody—not even the women in the family— what goes into it. But it's a Maui tradition. The delicious, sweet onions that come from Maui also have brought a sort of culinary fame to this island. They are known beyond our reefs simply as Maui onions. Raw, cooked or sauteed, they are arguably the best in the world, and found in local stores and markets. Another Maui tradition that's rapidly spreading comes from **Komoda Bakery** in Makawao, where the baked goods are sold the moment they're displayed. Hawai'i's governor buys his cream puffs here, as do other people who visit from Honolulu. Kitch'n

Cook'd Potato Chips, like the Maui onion, may be the best in the world. The supply is limited to ensure quality, and the chips are eagerly sought by visitors from other islands. They are found in Maui stores and markets, along with a gourmet version of the famous Maui potato chip. It's chocolate covered, and tasty.

The endemic treat that can't be packed and shipped home from Maui is 'shave ice'. Found throughout Hawai'i, this finely shaved ice with flavored syrup poured over it closely resembles the Mainland 'snow cone', but it isn't the same. The texture of shave ice is much finer—more like actual snow, and the rainbow version is a delight to behold as well as to consume. Some vendors will add a scoop of ice cream or sweet black beans under the mound of delicate ice shavings for a double treat. Shave ice can almost always be purchased from refreshment vans parked near beaches.

ACCOMMODATION

Resort hotels
Condominiums and apartments
Bed and breakfast
Cabins and campsites

ACCOMMODATION

O ne of the pleasures—and challenges—of traveling is finding the right place to stay. A comfortable room, suite or cottage can make a *good* trip a *great* one. The accommodations on Maui offer a broad spectrum of choices, from the posh resort hotels and all their amenities to the small condominiums and inns that often make up in price and charm what they may lack in grandeur. Most of the visitor accommodations are found in West Maui and along the southeast coast of Kīhei and Mākena. They range in price from a high of more than $200 a day down to something more modest. In this section we cover the top resort hotels on the island and list the major condominium units.

RESORT HOTELS

The ratings below indicate the quality of Maui's resort accommodations—a quality that is uniformly high. Accepting that the hotels will be clean and comfortable, our criteria goes on to include:
- architecture, decor, grounds and view
- a well-trained and responsive staff
- personal consideration from the manager, concierge, maitre d'hotel and staff
- amenities and niceties
- fine dining, convenient all-day restaurant
- on departure, the feeling that you'd want to return to this particular hotel

Unless you are traveling during the busy winter months (January through April with February at peak), reserving a room in advance should not be a problem.

Room rates are seasonal, with the winter months fetching higher prices. The price ranges of hotels are per day and categorized as follows:

$$$$	luxury class
$$$	$100-$200+
$$	$70-$100
$	$35-$70
No $	budget

NW   **No wheelchair access**

FIVE-STAR HOTELS

Hyatt Regency Ka'anapali $$$$

Elegant and luxurious, decorated with priceless Oriental art, this hotel features a spectacular pool, beautiful grounds with considerable birdlife (peacocks, parrots), and a lobby with a penguin pool. There are 815 rooms—including rooms for handicapped visitors—in three wings; four restaurants, including the five ★ Swan Court; health center; nightly entertainment and a discotheque. On Kā'anapali Beach, 200 Nohea Kai Drive, Lahaina 661-1234 (800 233-1234)

Kapalua Bay Hotel & Villas $$$$

This is the kind of resort that sets the standards for the others. It is a stunning showplace in northwest Maui situated in 750 acres of rural gentility, with a 194-room hotel, 125 villas, five fine-dining restaurants (two 5*), a tennis garden, two championship golf courses, shops, watersports—anything you need for a stay that is luxurious and complete. One Bay Drive, Kapalua 669-5656 (800 367-8000)

13

The Westin Maui $$$$

The Westin Maui is an oceanfront resort designed to complement nature. It features a vast complex of pools, streams and waterfalls which occupy the centerpiece of this 762-room hotel (including twenty-eight suites). There is a 25,000-square-foot pool area with five free-form pools and two waterslides, one of them 150 feet long. Guests can reserve seating at poolside. The hotel consists of two towers, which include three restaurants and six lounges. Also gracing this hotel is an art collection valued at $2 million from around the world. On Kā'anapali Beach, 2365 Kā'anapali Pkwy, Lahaina 667-2525

Hotel Hana-Maui $$$$ NW

The Hotel Hāna Maui is a jewel of a resort, in a class all its own. Breathtakingly luxurious, it still manages to hold tightly to its Hawaiian roots. The focal point of sleepy, beautiful Hāna, the resort is comprised of 97 bungalow-style guest rooms and suites spread over nearly sixty acres of rolling lawn. Original artwork and authentic Hawaiian artifacts are displayed in the main building, part of a $30 million renovation project. This Sheraton ITT resort has two pools and a private beach with guest facilities, a wellness center featuring exercise classes, equipment and consultation, massage facilities, two restaurants (one a five *) with selected menu items for health-conscious guests, and a staff that magically transforms into entertainers for evening dining. An 18-hole golf course in on the drawing boards for the future. P.O. Box 8, Hāna 248-8211 (800 325-3535)

ACCOMMODATION

Four Seasons Resort–Wailea $$$$ NW

An new elegant oceanfront resort with 380 rooms and an abundance of Pacific views. Three fine restaurants, live music at the Sunset Bar, two pools, tennis courts and access to Wailea's golf courses round out the appeal of this sparkling new hotel. 3900 Wailea Alanui 874-8000 (800 332-6284)

Grand Hyatt Wailea Resort & Spa $$$$ NW

This grand new resort has 787 rooms, all with ocean views, two pools the world's first water elevator, and a 50,000 square foot health spa operated by dedicated spa physicians. Five restaurants include one featuring spa cuisine, another, Japanese specialties. 3800 Wailea Ala Nui 875-1234 (800 233-1234)

FOUR-STAR HOTELS

Maui Marriott Resort $$$

A luxurious Kā'anapali Beach resort, this hotel offers 720 comfortable rooms, two pools, two spas and an exercise room. Four restaurants include one offering authentic Japanese cuisine; nightly entertainment plus a discotheque. On Kā'anapali Beach, 100 Nohea Kai Drive, Lahaina 667-1200 (800 542-6821/228-9290)

Maui Prince Hotel $$$$

The Maui Prince greets the sea with a graceful V-shaped structure in Mākena, the sunny southwest coast of Maui. There are carp ponds, a waterfall, a great courtyard that features chamber music, 300 rooms—some of which are designed for visitors with physical handicaps, two pools, four restaurants, the 18-hole Mākena Golf Course designed by Robert Trent Jones, Jr., six laykold tennis courts, and a sense of peace and privacy along with luxury. 5400 Mākena Alanui Road, Kihei 874-1111

Stouffer Wailea Beach Resort $$$

This hotel features gardens, waterfalls, pools and the luxurious tropical ambience for which many visitors come to Maui. All of the hotel's 347 rooms are large and liveable, including rooms for handicapped guests. There are three restaurants, including five ★ Raffles, a pool, music in the evenings and an excellent lu'au. 3550 Wailea Alanui Drive, Wailea 879-4900 (800 367-8047 x206)

Maui Inter-Continental Wailea $$$$

Sprawling and luxurious with gardens and the feel of the tropics, this hotel takes great advantage of its beachfront locale to conjure up an island paradise. The resort's 600 rooms make it one of the largest on Maui, but it loses nothing in expansiveness. There are three pools, a spa, four restaurants, five ★ dining at La Perouse, a good lū'au and a focus on Hawaiian arts and crafts in the decor. 3700 Wailea Alanui Drive, Wailea 879-1922 (800 367-2960)

THREE-STAR HOTELS

Embassy Suites $$$/$$$$ NW

This popular all-suite hotel is located on the beach in Kā'anapali. There are 397 one-bedroom and 16 two-bedroom suites. Guests are provided with full breakfasts, and cocktails from 4 till 6 p.m. nightly. There are two restaurants, and a pool with a waterslide. 104 Kā'anapali Parkway, Lahaina 661-2000

Ka'anapali Beach Hotel $$$ NW

This hotel prides itself on being "The Most Hawaiian Hotel," with a strong reputation for its Aloha Spirit. There are 430 rooms with excellent views in a convenient location, a pool, three restaurants and nightly entertainment. 2525 Kā'anapali Pkwy, Lahaina 661-0011 (800 657-7700)

Royal Lahaina Resort $$ NW

This hotel retains all of the charm it radiated when it opened. There are 514 rooms and cottages, all with the look and feel of the tropics, along with three pools, a spa, three restaurants, entertainment and a superb lū'au. On Kā'anapali Beach, 2780 Keka'a Drive, Lahaina 661-3611 (800 227-4700)

Sheraton-Maui Hotel $$$ NW

One of the more dramatic hotels on Maui, this establishment is adjacent to Kā'anapali Beach's Black Rock, and offers one of the best locations on the island for sun and water sports. The hotel has 500 rooms, two pools and two restaurants, and one of the best spots on Maui to watch a sunset—the Discovery Room Bar. There is a lū'au and entertainment. 2605 Kā'anapali Pkwy, Lahaina 661-0031 (800 325-3535)

CONDOMINIUMS and APARTMENTS

A more at-home atmosphere is available in self-contained apartments. They are plentiful and very popular, particularly for vacationers and business travelers staying several weeks. Apartment sizes vary, as do amenities, furnishings and prices. The price ranges shown are the same as those for hotels; there are many more units of this type available through real estate and property management agents on Maui, listed in the Yellow Pages under Real Estate Rentals.

CONDOMINIUMS and APARTMENTS

Colony Sands of Kahana ★★★★ $$$

On Kahana Bay, this high-rise condominium contains 200 spacious, sparkling one-, two- and three-bedroom units, with oceanfront lanais and furnished kitchens including microwave ovens. Front desk service is available 24 hours a day, and maid service is included. Other features include gardens, swimming pools, tennis courts, the Kahana Terrace Restaurant and lounge, a putting green and beachfront activities on a wide, white sand beach. 4299 HonoaPi'ilani Hwy, Lahaina 669-0400

Ka'anapali Ali'i ★★★★ $$$/$$$$

This luxury condominium consists of 264 one- and two-bedroom apartments, with 1500- to 1800-square feet of space. Concierge, maid service, 24-hour security and front desk service are available. The complex includes a swimming pool, a wading pool, saunas, a Jacuzzi, an exercise room, a restaurant and sundries. Kitchens are completely furnished including washer/dryer; tennis, golf. On Kā'anapali Beach, 50 Nohea Kai Drive, Lahaina 667-1400 (800 642-MAUI)

Aston Ka'anapali Shores Resort ★★★ $$$/$$$$

This is a tasteful beachfront condominium with 463 studios, one- and two-bedroom apartments and two-bedroom penthouses. The apartments are large, with quality furnishings and full-service kitchens. The condominium offers daily maid service, a 24-hour front desk, a lounge and restaurant, a swimming pool, beach services, 3 tennis courts. 3445 Lower Honoapi'ilani Road, Lahaina 667-2211 (800 922-7866)

Kama'ole Sands ★★★ $$$

This low-rise condominium resort features landscaped gardens overlooking Kama'ole Beach; 440 attractively furnished one-, two- and three-bedroom suites; front desk and daily maid service; and fully-equipped kitchens. Other amenities include a clubhouse, four tennis courts, swimming pool, Jacuzzi, barbecue areas with tables and benches. Five minutes away from Wailea Resort and golf courses. 2695 S Kīhei Road, Kīhei 874-8700

Wailea Condominiums ★★★ $$-$$$$

Three condominium complexes—**Ekahi**, **Elua** and **Ekolu**—make up the 500 luxurious units in Wailea. Beachfront Wailea-Elua has won awards in landscaping and architecture. Low-rise units include studios and one-, two- and three-bedroom apartments with *lānais*, expensive furnishings, complete kitchens including washer/dryer and daily maid service. Ten restaurants, two golf courses, eight swimming pools, fourteen tennis courts are located here. 3750 Wailea Alanui Place, Wailea 879-1595 (800 367-5246)

Whaler on Ka'anapali Beach ★★★ $$$/$$$$

This is the first condominium established on Kā'anapali Beach. The complex, which was recently renovated, features big, oceanfront studios and one- and two-bedroom units with spacious private *lānais* and both garden and ocean views. Cheery decor with rattan and wicker furnishings fill the rooms, which also include fully-equipped kitchens. Maid service, around-the-clock front desk,

CONDOMINIUMS and APARTMENTS

swimming pool, sauna, exercise room, four tennis courts and two paddle tennis courts are included. 2481 Kā'anapali Pkwy 661-4861 (US 800 367-7052; West Canada 800 663-1118; East Canada 800 268-1734)

Aston Maui Lu Resort ☆☆ $$

On the beach at Mā'alaea Bay, these 180 studios and one- and two-bedroom cottages are in an open-air, palm garden setting that features authentic Hawaiian hospitality. Amenities include restaurant, lounge, swimming pool, beach activities, tennis courts and golf nearby. The lu'au is old-style Hawaiian with a full *imu* ceremony. 575 S Kīhei Road, Kīhei 879-5881 (US 800 367-5244; interisland 800 592-3351)

Mana Kai Maui Resort ☆☆ $$/$$$

On the beach in Kīhei, this resort has 98 bedrooms and one- and two-bedroom apartments which come with free use of a car. Completely furnished kitchens, maid service and front desk service are included. The complex also has a restaurant, cocktail lounge, swimming pool and meeting room. 2960 S Kīhei Road, Kīhei 879-1561 (800 525-2025)

Maui Eldorado Resort Condominium ☆☆ $$$

Overlooking Kā'anapali Golf Course, just a walk away from Kā'anapali Beach Resort, this low-rise condominium consists of 204 studios, one-bedroom apartments and two-bedroom suites set amidst gardens and swimming pools. The resort provides transportation to the beach and a beach activities desk for guests. Golf and tennis facilities are available. 2661 Keka'a Drive, Lahaina 661-0021 (US 800 367-2967; interisland 800 542-6825; Canada 800 663-1118)

Maui Hill Resort ☆☆ $$$

On the Kīhei Coast, just minutes from Wailea and a walk to the beach, these 140 furnished one-, two- and three-bedroom apartments are set in garden surroundings. *Lānai*s offer an ocean view, and the rooms include modern kitchens complete with microwave ovens and maid service. Tennis courts, putting green, swimming pool and sundeck are available, and golfers may tee off at the adjacent Wailea Resort. 2881 S Kīhei Road, Kīhei 879-6321

Napili Kai Beach Club ☆☆ $$/$$$

Guests return season after season to this oldest West Maui hotel that offers 136 ocean-view or oceanfront rooms in two-story buildings. Each unit includes a kitchenette. The Sea House Restaurant has nightly entertainment. Other features are five swimming pools, a large Jacuzzi, tennis courts, shuffleboard and the Kapalua Golf Course two minutes away. Nāpili Bay, 5900 HonoaPi'ilani Hwy, Lahaina 669-6271 (800 367-5030)

Napili Shores Resort ☆☆ $$/$$$

The 152 studios and one-bedroom condominium units overlook Napili Bay and include furnished kitchens and lanais. The complex also has front desk and maid service, two swimming pools, a Jacuzzi, laundromat and a store. Golf and tennis may be played at nearby Kapalua Bay Hotel. 5315 HonoaPi'ilani Hwy, Lahaina 669-8061 (800 367-6046)

CONDOMINIUMS and APARTMENTS

Papakea Beach Resort ★★ $$$

This condominium is set on Honokōwai beachfront property, at the edge of Kā'anapali. The low-rise condominium includes 300 studios, and one- and two-bedroom units surrounded by pools and gardens. Lānais, full-service kitchens, ceiling fans, front desk and maid service are included. Other features are lighted tennis courts with a resident pro, two swimming pools and Jacuzzis, saunas, shuffleboard courts, two putting greens and barbecue areas. 3543 HonoaPi'ilani Hwy, Lahaina 669-4848 (800 367-7052)

Aston Mahana at Ka'anapali ★★ $$

Every condominium unit is beachfront. Luxury studio, 1 and 2 bedroom/2 bath suites, pool, fully equipped kitchens, and a Gourmet Sundry Store. 110 Kā'anapali Shores Place 661-8751 (800 922-7866)

Pioneer Inn ★★ $

142

Maui's oldest hotel with sections dating back to 1901, this green and white inn is famous, and marks the center of Lahaina activity. The hotel consists of 48 rooms, the older ones full of character. One long veranda overlooks the harbor. The new, more modern wing was built in 1965, and its rooms have private lānais overlooking the courtyard. Memorabilia fills the lobby, and the open-air bar is popular among Maui residents. The hotel also includes a restaurant and shops lining the downstairs. 658 Wharf Street, Lahaina 661-3636

The Lahaina Hotel ★★ $$$ NW

The old hotel never had it so good—even in Lahaina's hey-day! This restored spot just off Front Street welcomes the visitor with turn of the century warmth. Authentic Victorian antiques and beautifully chosen decor is a striking contrast to the ultra-contemporary accommodations elsewhere on the island. Crazy Shirts' founder Rick Ralston, who owns the hotel, has taken great pains to make it a landmark. Private baths and balconies. 127 Lahainaluna St., Lahaina 661-0577

BED and BREAKFAST

Some visitors may want to try the increasingly popular option of staying in a Bed and Breakfast, the old-world tradition with many modern variations. On Maui there are dozens available; prices range from thirty dollars per night for a single to sixty dollars and up for a double. Though available throughout the island, many are concen-trated in Upcountry, off the usual tourist path, and affording a closer look at Maui's people and lifestyles.

Bed & Breakfast Connections Maui Style (879-7865) and **Bed & Breakfast Hawai'i** (800 347-6548) offer listings for the cottages and other B & B facilities on Maui as well as other islands.

CABINS and CAMPSITES

Maui County maintains two campgrounds for tents and auto campers. One is **Baldwin Park** on the Hāna Highway near the town of Pā'ia, a beach-side park that has water, showers, restrooms, grills and tables. The second is **Rainbow Park** on Baldwin Avenue just above Pā'ia, a more woodsy setting that has everything Baldwin Park has, minus the showers. You must get a permit to stay at either park, and the permits limit your stay to three consecutive nights, and fifteen nights per year. The fee is three dollars for adults, fifty cents for children. Permits are obtained from the County's Parks and Recreation Department (243-7230), located at the War Memorial Gym, Ka'ahumanu Avenue, Wailuku 96793. The Department is open Monday through Friday, 8am to 4pm.

The state of Hawai'i provides three campgrounds, each with its particular charm. **Kaumahina State Wayside Park** on the Hāna Highway offers tent-camping with a view, and peaceful surroundings; it is about thirty miles from Wailuku. A second site is at **Wai'ānapanapa** (see SIGHTSEEING and BEACHES), a remote beach in Hāna. A third site, isolated in a thick grove of hardwood trees and reachable by four-wheel drive, is at **Polipoli Springs**, just above the 6000-foot level on the side of Haleakalā. This is a demanding place to get to, and once there, you are removed from amenities, so don't forget anything essential. You will see striking views of Maui enroute to Polipoli. There is no fee for camping in state parks, but permits are required and the maximum stay is five nights. For permits, contact the Division of State Parks, PO Box 1049, State Office Building, Wailuku 96793 (244-4354).

The state of Hawai'i also manages cabins at two locations. They are bargains—good facilities at reasonable prices. Permits are necessary from the State Parks office (above) and length of stay limited. Make reservations well ahead of time. Wai'ānapanapa has twelve cabins, which are very comfortable and well-furnished with bedding, towels, cooking and eating gear, hot water, showers, refrigerators and electric stoves. Each cabin will accommodate up to six people at a maximum cost of thirty dollars per night. Polipoli has a single cabin, with all the furnishings of Wai'ānapanapa except electricity. It has a gas stove instead. The cabin can lodge up to ten people at a maximum charge of fifty dollars per night.

The US National Park Service provides campgrounds and cabins inside Haleakalā National Park (see SIGHTSEEING), surely among the most spectacular campsites anywhere in the world. One campsite is at **Hosmer Grove**, at the 7000-foot level. No permit is necessary here, and facilities are on a first-come, first-served basis. The site has shelter, parking area, grills and tables both in the shelter and outside.

Two campsites adjacent to cabins operated by the Park Service are located inside the crater. The sites are at the **Hōlua cabin**, the first one encountered when hiking or riding in the park, and at **Palikū**, the most distant cabin. Tent camping here is limited to three nights, and to twenty-five persons per campsite.

The sites are seldom full, however. A third campsite is at the extreme end of the park on the Hāna coast, at **'Ohe'o**. This latter site is relatively undeveloped and there is no water. There is no fee for camping at any of the sites, but permits are necessary from Park Headquarters (572-9306) and/or by writing: Superintendent, Haleakalā National Park, PO Box 369, Makawao 96768.

In addition to the Hōlua and Palikū cabins noted above, there is a third cabin, **Kapalaoa**, and all three are extremely popular with residents and visitors alike. Permits are necessary from Park Headquarters (above) which is open 8:30am to 4pm daily. The cabins are warm and cozy, and equipped with water, toilets, wood-burning stove, firewood and cooking and eating utensils. There are mattresses but no bedding, and it is necessary to bring a warm sleeping bag. The cabins hold a minimum of three, a maximum of twelve, which means most parties share the cabins with other groups. Fees for the cabins are five dollars per person per night, plus two dollars and fifty cents for firewood, for a total of seven fifty per night each.

Because of the popularity of the cabins, they are in great demand. Those who would like to stay in them must write the Superintendent (above), and give details on exact dates and cabins desired, and the number of people in your group. A lottery is then held to determine who gets to stay in the cabins; the lottery is held generally two months ahead, meaning your reservations should be in at least ninety days before your proposed adventure.

Camping, hiking, or just visiting Haleakalā is an experience long remembered. The crater is one of the world's great scenic wonders, and a spiritual place for Maui's original inhabitants. Visitors should respect the land by practicing good trail habits and forbidding litter.

Interestingly enough, an old Hawaiian legend about Haleakalā almost has been lost in time; even today's Hawaiian would be surprised to find that the old Polynesian settlers had, in their pantheon of gods, four sisters who were goddesses of the snows. This legend is easy to believe on some winter mornings when the park is closed by snow. The four snow goddesses came from far over the sea and were rivals of Pele, the goddess of fire, who lived in the volcanoes. An old Hawaiian tale talks of the fierce battles between Pele and the paramount snow goddess, Poli'ahu. She always won the battles because at the end of the fiery eruptions caused by Pele, the gentle snow would still fall like a white mantle over the summits of the volcanoes. The goddess who was said to live in Haleakalā was Līlīnoe, and on dark, blustery nights in the crater, it is easy to believe she still watches over her beloved Haleakalā.

ET CETERA

Other services
Traveling with children
Handicapped travelers
Other islands

146

OTHER SERVICES

H ere we cover a miscellany of other services that did not lend themselves to appropriate inclusion in other sections of the guidebook—everything from typists to luggage repair to specialists in the arrangement of tropical nuptials.

POST OFFICES

Maui's Post Offices are located throughout the island, but working hours vary from site to site. In general they are Monday through Friday 8:00am-4:30pm, Saturday 8:00am-12noon. They are located at:
Ha'ikū (575-2773) 96708
Hāna (248-8258) 96713
Kahului (871-4710) 96732
Kīhei (879-2403) 96753
Kula (878-1765) 96790
Makawao (572-8895) 96768
Pā'ia (579-8205) 96779
Pukalani (572-8235) 96768
Pu'unēnē (871-4744) 96784
Wailuku (244-4815) 96793
Lahaina, main (667-6611) 96761
Lahaina, downtown (661-0550) 96761

PUBLICATIONS

Publications that may be of interest to visitors include the *Maui News* (244-3981), an afternoon newspaper that is printed every day except Saturday; *Pacific Art & Travel*, published quarterly and focusing on Hawaii's art scene; *Real Estate Maui Style*, published monthly, and free tourist guides found in racks island-wide.

LEATHER GOODS-REPAIRS

If your luggage or shoes need fixing, you are limited to taking them to **Lahaina Shoe & Luggage Repair** (661-3114) in Lahaina; they handle repairs while you wait. **Tester's Shoe Repair** (877-7140) in the Old Kahului Store is convenient for Central Valley residents.

WEDDINGS

Maui is just as popular an island for weddings or renewing vows as any other in the Hawaiian chain. A local firm specializing in making dream weddings happen here is **A Hawaiian Wedding Experience** (667-6689), with offices on three islands, and on Maui, in Lahaina. Similarly, **Weddings the Maui Way** (877-7711) and **Maui Inter-Continental Wailea** (879-1922) offer complete services.

LAUNDROMATS and DRY CLEANERS

Dodd Dry Cleaners (244-5121), Snow White Linen/Laundry (871-0633), Fabritek Cleaners (877-4444), Paia Clothes Cleaners (579-9273), and Valley Isle Dry Cleaning Laundry and Valet (877-4411), offer full-service laundry service. For self-service laundries there are Cabanilla Kwik 'n Kleen (667-5182) in Lahaina, W&F Washerette (877-0353) in Kahului, and The Washtub (572-1654) in the Pukalani Terrace Center.

TRAVELING WITH CHILDREN

Warm and welcoming Maui is an excellent place to bring children on vacation. The near-perfect climate allows children to spend time outdoors at the beach or in a park. In addition, several resort hotels organize excursions and tours just for children. An example is the **Kamp Hyatt** program sponsored by **Hyatt Regency Kā'anapali** for children ages five to twelve. They visit Lahaina and other historic sites, and ride the Sugarcane Train on one tour; a second takes them on a catamaran ride on the *Kiele V*; still another teaches them about Hawai'i's customs and traditions. Parents may make reservations for their children through the hotel's Recreation Department (667-7474). Other hotels feature similar programs, though they may be seasonal. The concierge or hotel activities desk can arrange your

Maori-designed mailbox, Hāna..

TRAVELING WITH CHILDREN

child's participation.

High quality clothes suitable for Maui—baby T-shirts, tank tops and visors--are available at **Baby's Choice** in Maui Mall Center.

Youngsters are fascinated by the imposing skeleton of a sperm whale in the **Whaler's Village Whaling Museum**. **Superwhale**, in Whaler's Village and in Lahaina Cannery, also carries fashions for children.

HANDICAPPED TRAVELERS

T he State's Commission on the Handicapped publishes 'The Maui Travelers Guide for Physically Handicapped Persons', a useful guide for handicapped travelers. While the brochure does not endorse particular hotels or restaurants, it does indicate which establishments have wheelchair access, handicapped parking stalls and lowered telephone booths. Call the Commission (244-4441), or write: Commission on the Handicapped, State Department of Health, 54 High Street, Wailuku 96793.

TRANSPORTATION

Maui has no public transportation system, hence no system designed particularly for handicapped travelers. There are private taxis and car rentals available, but the Commission notes they can accommodate only the partially disabled and the ambulatory traveler. Of the car rental companies on Maui, Avis and Hertz can install hand-controls, but a request for this should be made as far in advance as possible to **Avis Rent A Car** (871-7575) or **Hertz Rent A Car** (877-5167).

SUPPORT SERVICES

Some Maui agencies offer personal care attendants, nurse aides, health aides and volunteer companions. **Maui Center for Independent Living** (242-4966) provides personal care attendants. Other helpful service organizations are **Akamai Nursing Service** (878-6125) and **Medical Personnel Pool** (877-2676).

MEDICAL EQUIPMENT

These firms on Maui rent out medical equipment for the physically disabled: **GASPRO** (877-0056), at 365 Hanakai Street, Kahului, and **Maui Medical Equipment** (877-4032) at 355 Hukilike St., #103, also in Kahului. **Medicare Supply Services** in Lahaina (661-8339), Kahului (877-6222), and Kihei (874-0460) offers a 24-hour hotline and will deliver.

RECREATION

The **Maui Easter Seal Society** (877-4443) can help arrange recreational activities for handicapped people, including wheelchair tennis and basketball, bowling and swim classes.

ACCESS

Most major shopping malls, major dining establishments and showrooms provide handicapped parking, wheelchair access, adapted restrooms and lowered telephone booths. The Commission on the Handicapped suggests checking with such places in advance. Additionally, there are several hotels that have large rooms to serve physically handicapped persons. To find out about access at condominiums, contact the Commission or the condominium directly.

The notation **NW** is used in the ACCOMMODATION and DINING sections of this book to denote those establishments that do not have wheelchair access.

OTHER ISLANDS

V isitors occasionally are surprised to find that the county of Maui consists of four islands: Maui, Moloka'i, Lāna'i and Kaho'olawe, owned by the US government and accessible only with US Navy permission. The county—the second largest in the state—consists of 1174 square miles [3042 sq km] of land and about 90,000 people.

Beacuse each of the main Hawaiian islands is unique and has so much to offer, the same in-depth coverage in this book is provided in *The Essential Guide to O'ahu*, *The Essential Guide to Kaua'i*, and *The Essential Guide to Hawai'i, the Big Island*. Interisland airlines are Aloha Airlines, Hawaiian Airlines, Panorama Air, Princeville Airways and Air Molokai.

MOLOKA'I

Moloka'i and her people embody much of the traditional Hawaiian spirit, and prefer to keep to the old ways as much as possible. Somnolent and slow, Moloka'i has a handful of hotels and remains uncrowded. The northwestern coast contains the peninsula where, in the 1860s, those suffering from leprosy were forced ashore in isolation. The settlement of Kalaupapa today is still the home of a dwindling (less than 200) number of those afflicted with Hansen's disease. Remote, wind-swept and silent, Kalaupapa receives an occasional visitor.

The primary contact for such visits is the sheriff, James Brede (567-6171). Visitors also may make arrangements through one of the commuter airlines. Kalaupapa contains a memorial to the Belgian priest, Father Damien, who died a martyr serving the lepers on the lonely peninsula.

LĀNA'I

The rural island of Lanai also seems to be caught in another time. Owned almost entirely by Castle & Cooke, the island is extensively planted in pineapple, the only major industry for many years until the opening of two new resort hotels, the Lodge at Koele (565-7231) and the Manele Bay Hotel (565-7231). Both are elegant luxury hotels, the former being a quiet country estate, the latter a splendid full-service resort on the cliffs over looking Manele Bay. The charming old-style Hotel Lanai is also available in Lanai City (565-7211). All the Lanai hotels offer shuttle service from the airport. Lanai's Manele Bay is a lovely natural bay with plenty of colorful underwater life to explore. Another scenic spot is a strange sculpture garden called "Garden of the Gods." Commuter airlines fly between Maui and Lanai. Four-wheel-drive vehicles can be rented from one of several car rental agencies on the island.

O'AHU

Beyond the county of Maui lies the island of O'ahu, seat of government, capital of the state of Hawai'i and called, with reason, 'the Gathering Place'. Some seventy-five percent of the State's population of more than one million is found on O'ahu. The island combines a modern, urban atmosphere with its beautiful tropical setting; Honolulu is as up-to-date as any other leading city of the world. O'ahu is the site of Pearl Harbor and other major US military installations and commands.

KAUA'I

One hundred miles northwest of O'ahu is the oldest inhabited island in the chain, Kaua'i. Known as 'the Garden Isle', Kaua'i is an island of flowers and slow ways, but highly experienced in handling masses of visitors while protecting this breathtaking paradise.

Hanalei is one of the world's most beautiful valleys, and is located at the north of the island.

The spectacular Waimea Canyon tends to dwarf everything else on the island. Called the 'Grand Canyon of the Pacific', it is not quite as large as its namesake, but is every bit as stunning.

NI'IHAU

The island of Ni'ihau, as noted earlier, is privately owned. Seventeen miles from Kaua'i, it has been removed from mainstream Hawai'i for decades. The Robinson family of Kaua'i has kept the island as a place where Hawaiians, if they chose, could live a traditional lifestyle. Most residents never leave the island. The spoken language is Hawaiian. Until recently, voting in elections meant the people of Ni'ihau had to send their ballots via boat through the surf to Kaua'i to be counted. The only

Hāna's magical moodiness.

authorized visits to Ni'ihau are those by a few state government leaders who go to assure themselves that educational funds and other state monies are being properly dispensed and used. Recently, scenic helicopter flights over the island began. Landing at a designated spot has been approved, but no contact with residents is allowed.

HAWAI'I

The remaining inhabited island is the largest and youngest of them all, the island of Hawai'i. 'The Big Island' is so big that all the other islands would fit into its borders, with room to spare. Five major volcanoes built the island of Hawai'i, and one of them, Kīlauea on the flanks of Mauna Loa, continues an eruptive cycle that is still building the coastline. The island of Hawai'i is a place of great variety, from the sleepy plantation-town atmosphere of East Hawai'i to the tropical, but bustling, West Hawai'i side. In the center of the island are the two highest peaks in the Pacific, Mauna Kea and Mauna Loa, each almost 14,000 feet. Here too is the enormous and privately owned Parker Ranch, more than 200,000 acres dotted with beautiful, healthy cattle. The Big Island was the birthplace of the conqueror, Kamehameha the Great, who united the islands into one kingdom. The monarch died in Kona and his remains are hidden forever, as was the custom for great leaders in Hawai'i.

MORE ISLANDS

There are other islands in the Hawaiian archipelago, but the average visitor is not likely to see them. They are the more than hundred shoals, sand bars and islets that stretch from the Big Island northwest to tiny Kure Island, above Midway, more than 1500 miles away. Parts of them are wildlife sanctuaries.

Uncharted reefs have ripped out the bottoms of unsuspecting ships. One such island complex is French Frigate Shoals, for years a US installation for navigation and weather reporting.

LO'IHI

A million or so years from now, the visitor here is likely to find a new Hawaiian island. If the underwater eruption south of the Big Island keeps going at its present rate, another island will be created. Scientists who have seen the undersea eruption with its sea mount beginning to form have given it a name—Lo'ihi, a word which means long, or tall, or prolonged in time.

APPENDIX

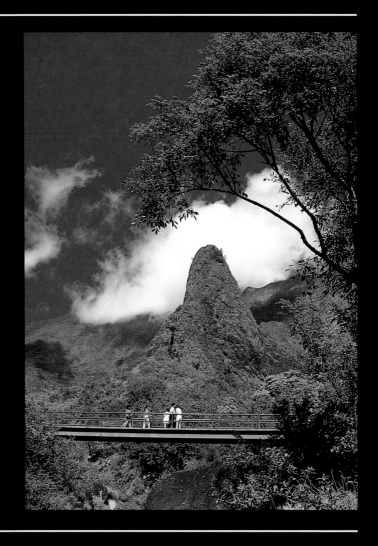

PLACES OF INTEREST

LAHAINA/KA'ANAPALI

Baldwin Home Museum
688 Front St 661-3262
Banyan Tree
by Hotel St in Lahaina
Black Rock
Sheraton-Maui Hotel (661-0031)
Brick Palace
near Hauola Stone, front of Lahaina
Library
The Carthaginian
end of Papelekane St, across from
Pioneer Inn
Coral Miracle Church
see St Gabriel's Church
Coral Stone House
see Richards, William, home of
Hale Pa'i, the Printing House
adjacent to Lahainaluna High
School 667-7040
Hale Pa'ahao
Waine'e St, opposite corner of David
Malo's home
Hauola Stone
north of *The Carthaginian*
Lahaina Hongwanji Mission
551 Waine'e St 661-0640
Lahaina Jodo Mission
12 Ala Moana, near Māla Wharf
661-4304
Lahaina Restoration Foundation
661-3262
Lahainaluna High School
980 Lahainaluna Rd 661-0313
Malu'uluoLele Park
corner of Front and Shaw Sts
Masters' Reading Room
Front St between Dickenson and
Papelekane Sts 661-3334
Mt Ball
above Lahainaluna High School
near giant 'L'
Old Fort
next to Old Lahaina Courthouse

Old Lahaina Courthouse
Wharf St 661-0970
Pioneer Inn
behind *The Carthaginian* 661-3636
Richards, William, home of
near Masters' Reading
Room 244-3326
Rotten Row
end of Wharf St
Shingon Temple
Luakini St
Waine'e Cemetery
535 Waine'e St
Waiola Church
535 Waine'e St 661-4349
Whalers Village Museum
Whalers Village 661-5992

KIHEI/WAILEA

'Āhihi-Kīna'u Natural Area Reserve
Mākena
Bellstone
by Nākālele Pt
La Perouse Bay
south of 'Āhihi-Kīna'u Natural
Area Reserve

HANA

Hale Waiwai O Hāna
see Hāna Cultural Center
Hāna Cultural Center
near turnoff to Hāna Bay 248-8622
Hasegawa General Store
Hāna Hwy 248-8231
Helani Gardens
Hāna Hwy 248-8274
Ka'uiki Head
area in Hāna
Ke'anae Arboretum
above Hwy 36 248-8592

Ke'anae Valley Lookout
Hwy 36
Kuialoha Church
Hwy 36, Kaupō
Mantokuji Buddhist Temple
Pā'ia
Palapala Ho'omau Church
by Kīpahulu Ranch
Pi'ilanihale Heiau
Alaino Rd
St Gabriel's Church
Wailua
Seven Pools
road past Hāna
Wānanalua Church
corner of Hāna Hwy and Hauoli St
248-8040

UPCOUNTRY

Church of the Holy Ghost
hillside above Waiakoa
Haleakalā National Park
Visitor Center 572-7749
Kula Botanical Gardens
Upper Kula Rd 878-1715
Leleiwi Overlook
9000-foot level of Haleakalā
Pā'ia sugar mill
Baldwin Ave
Park Headquarters
Haleakalā National Park, 7000-foot
level, a mile inside the park en-
trance 572-9306
Pu'u 'Ula'ula, Red Hill
Visitor Center
top of Haleakalā

Tedeschi Vineyards, Ltd
Hwy 37, 'Ulupalakua 878-6058
'Ulupalakua Ranch
Hwy 37 near Kēōkea 878-1202
UH College of Tropical Agriculture
Experimental Station
off Hwy 37 onto Copp Rd, south of
Kula Elementary School

WAILUKU-KAHULUI

Bailey House Museum
2375A Main St 244-3326
Haleki'i Heiau
Kūhiō Pl.
Ka'ahumanu Church
High St 244-5189
Kalana O Maui, County Building
High St 244-7711
Kanahā Pond
between Kahului Airport and
Wailuku
Kepaniwai Heritage Gardens
road to 'Iao Valley 244-3656
Maui Historical Society Museum
2375A Main St 244-3326
Maui Tropical Plantation
High St, Hwy 30 at Waikapū
244-7643
Pali 'Ele'ele
Iao Valley State Park
Pihana Heiau
Kūhiō Pl.
Sugar Plant
by Kahului Harbor
Wailuku Library
251 High St 244-3945

RESTAURANTS

AMERICAN

Avalon Restaurant & Bar
Mariner's Alley, Lahaina 667-5559
Buzz's Wharf
Maalaea Bay 244-5426
The Chart House
500 N Pu'unēnē Ave, Kahului
877-2476
1450 Front St., Lahaina 661-0987
Chuck's Steakhouse
Kīhei Town Center 879-4488
Cook's at the Beach
Westin Maui, Kā'anapali 667-2525
David Paul's Lahaina Grill
127 Lahainaluna Road 667-5117
Denny's
Lahaina Square Ctr 667-7898,
Kamaole Shopping Ctr, Kīhei
879-0604
Haliimaile General Store
900 Haliimaile Road 572-2666
Hard Rock Cafe
Lahaina Center 667-7400
Hotel Hāna-Maui
Hotel Hāna-Maui 248-8211
Kapalua Grill & Bar
200 Kapalua Dr. 669-5653
Kimo's
845 Front St, Lahaina 661-4811
Kula Lodge
Haleakalā Hwy 878-1535
Leilani's on the Beach
Whalers Village, Kā'anapali
661-4495
Makawao Steak & Fish House
3612 Baldwin Ave, Makawao
572-8711
Market Cafe
Kapalua Shops, Kapalua Bay
Resort 669-4888
Maui Rose
Embassy Suites, Kā'anapali
661-2000

Moose McGillycuddy's
Mariner's Alley, Lahaina 667-7758
Nanatomi
Seafood and Steak Restaurant
Kā'anapali Pkwy 667-7902
Ocean Terrace
Mana Kai Maui
2960 So. Kīhei Road 879-2607
Pioneer Inn
Lahaina Harborfront 661-3636
The Plantation Veranda
Kapalua Bay Resort 669-5656
Prince Court
Maui Prince Hotel, Mākena
874-1111
The Rusty Harpoon Restaurant
Whalers Village, Kā'anapali
661-3123
Sam's Beachside Grill
505 Front Street, Lahaina 667-4341
Sandcastle at Wailea
Wailea Shopping Village 879-0606
Set Point Cafe
Wailea Tennis Club 879-3244

CHINESE

China Boat
4474 Lower Honoa Pi'ilani Road
669-5089
Chopsticks
Royal Lahaina Resort 661-3611
Fu Wah
Pukalani Terrace Ctr, Up Country
572-1341
Ming Yuen
162 Alamaha St, Kahului 871-7787

CONTINENTAL

Garden Restaurant
Kapalua Bay Resort 669-0244
Lahaina Provision Company
Hyatt Regency Kā'anapali,
Kā'anapali 661-1234

Pineapple Hill
1000 Kapalua Dr. 669-6129
Raffles
Stouffer Wailea Beach Resort
879-4900
Sound of the Falls
Westin Maui, Kā'anapali 667-2525
Swan Court
Hyatt Regency Kā'anapali,
Kā'anapali 667-1234

FRENCH

Chez Paul
820-B Olowalu Village 661-3843
Gerard's
174 Lahainaluna Rd, Lahaina
661-8939
La Bretagne
562-C Front St., Lahaina 661-8966
La Perouse
Maui Inter-Continental Wailea
879-1922

ITALIAN

Alex's Hole in the Wall
834 Front St, Lahaina 661-3197
Casanova Italian Deli
1188 Makawao Ave 572-0220
Longhi's
888 Front St, Lahaina 667-2288
Luigi's Pasta & Pizza
Maui Mall, Kahului 877-3761
Spats
Hyatt Regency Kā'anapali,
Kā'anapali 667-1234

JAPANESE

Hakone
Maui Prince Hotel, Mākena
874-1111
Kobe Steak House
136 Dickenson St, Lahaina
667-5555
Nikko Steakhouse Maui
Marriott Hotel, Kā'anapali
667-1200

SEAFOOD

The Bay Club
Kapalua Bay Resort 669-5656
Bettino's Restaurant & Lounge
505 Front St., Lahaina 661-8810
El Crab Catcher
Whalers Village, Kā'anapali
661-4423
Erik's Seafood Broiler
Kamaole Shopping Ctr, Kīhei
879-8400
Erik's Seafood Grotto
Kahana Villas Condos 669-4806
Island Fish House
1945 S. Kihei Road 879-7771
Kihei Prime Rib & Seafood House
2511 S. Kihei Road 879-1954
Mama's Fish House
799 Kaiholo Pl. 579-9672
Mango Jones
2550 Kekaa Drive 667-6847
Mickey's
33 Lono Ave, Kahului 871-7555
Rainbow Lagoon Restaurant
Rainbow Mall, Kihei 879-5600
Sea House Restaurant
5900 HonoaPi'ilani Hwy, Nāpili
669-6271

THAI

Island Thai
1280 S. Kihei Rd., Kihei 874-0813
Orient Express
Napili Shores Resort 669-8077
Siam Thai
123 N Market St, Wailuku
244-3817

MISCELLANEOUS

Grandma's Maui Coffee
Upcountry 878-2140
Komoda Bakery
Makawao 572-7261
Pukalani Terrace Country
Clubhouse Restaurant
Pukalani Golf Course 572-1325
Tasaka Guri Guri
Maui Mall 871-4513

SHOPPING

SHOPPING CENTERS

Azeka Place
1280 S Kīhei Rd, Kīhei 879-8400
Dolphin Plaza
2395 S. Kīhei Rd, Kīhei
505 Front Street
near the Banyan Tree, Lahaina
667-2514
Gateway Shopping Center
Lower HonoaPi'ilani Rd, Kahana
Kaahumanu Shopping Center
Ka'ahumanu Ave, Kahului
877-3369
Kahului Shopping Center
Ka'ahumanu Ave, Kahului
877-5527
Kamaole Shopping Center
S Kīhei Rd, between Kama'ole
Beach Park I and II
Kapalua Shops
adjacent to Kapalua Bay Hotel
(669-5656)
Kihei Town Center
1881 S. Kīhei Road
Kukui Mall
1819 S. Kīhei Road
Lahaina Cannery Shopping Center
1221 HonoaPi'ilani Hwy,
Lahaina 661-5304
Lahaina Center
corner of Papalaua St & Front St,
Lahaina
Lahaina Market Place
corner of Front St and Lahainaluna
Rd, Lahaina 667-2636
Lahaina Shopping Center
Front St, Lahaina 924-1000 (Hono #)
Lahaina Square Shopping Center
2145 Wells St., Lahaina 242-4400
Mariner's Alley
844 Front St, Lahaina 661-8351
Maui Mall Shopping Center
Ka'ahumanu Ave, Kahului
877-5523

Pukalani Terrace Center
Haleakalā Hwy (Route 36, 37),
Upcountry 572-7900
Rainbow Mall
2439 S Kīhei Rd, Kīhei 879-6144
Wailea Shopping Village
3750 Wailea Alanui Dr. 879-4474
Whalers Village
Kā'anapali Pkwy, Kā'anapali
661-4567
The Wharf
opposite the Banyan Tree,
658 Front St., Lahaina 661-8748

SHOPS

A to Z Stores
770 Front St, Lahaina 667-9357,
816A Front St, Lahaina 661-5089,
4401 HonoaPi'ilani Hwy, Nāpili
669-0080, Banyan Inn, Lahaina
661-3901
A-1 Pineapples
380 Dairy Rd, Kahului 877-3135
ABC Discount Stores
Lahaina Cannery Ctr 661-5370,
Whalers Village 667-9700,
724 Front St, Lahaina 667-9558,
2349 Kīhei Rd, Kīhei 879-6305
3511 HonoaPi'ilani Hwy, Nāpili
669-0271, 888 Front St, Lahaina
661-5324
ACA Joe
Whaler's Village 667-2282
Ah Fook's Super Market
Kahului Shopping Ctr 877-3308
Airport Flower & Fruit
460 Dairy Rd, Kahului 871-7056,
877-6131, 640 Front St, Lahaina
667-7463
Andrade
Sheraton-Maui Hotel 661-0031/
8544 (and other locations)

Apparels of Pauline
Lahaina Market Place 661-4774
Arabesque
Lahaina Cannery Ctr 667-5337
Azeka's Market
Azeka Place 879-0611
Baby's Choice
Maui Mall 877-6022
Ben Franklin
Ka'ahumanu Ctr 877-3337,
Lahaina Shopping Ctr 661-0076
(and other locations)
Benetton
Whalers Village 661-8188
Cactus Tree
Kukui Mall, Kihei 874-0883
Center Art Galleries
802 Front St, Lahaina 661-1250,
Hyatt Regency Kā'anapali,
Kā'anapali 661-1200 (and other
locations)
Claire, the Ring Lady
858-4 Front St, Lahaina 667-9288
The Clothes Addict
12 Baldwin Ave, Pā'ia 579-9266
Coast Gallery
Intercontinental Hotel, Wailea
879-2301
Coral Grotto
Sheraton-Maui Hotel, Kā'anapali
661-4007, Pioneer Inn, Lahaina
661-4652
The Curtis Wilson Cost Gallery
Kula Lodge, Upcountry 878-6544
Crazy Shirts
Lahaina Cannery Ctr 661-4788,
865 Front St, Lahaina 661-4775,
The Wharf 661-4712,
Azeka Place 879-8577, Whaler's
Village 661-0117
Depot Gift Shop
Sugarcane Train Depot, Lahaina
661-5786
Dolphin Galleries
Whalers Village 661-5115,
Lahaina Cannery Ctr 661-5000
Larry Dotson Gallery & Studio
143 Lahainaluna Rd, Lahaina
661-3838

Down to Earth
1910 Vineyard Blvd, Wailuku
242-6821
Dyansen Gallery of Maui
Kā'anapali Pkwy 667-2002,
Mariner's Alley 661-2055
Eelskin Factory Outlet
764 Front St, Lahaina 661-0602,
11 Market St, Wailuku 242-5546
Elephant Walk
Hyatt Regency Kā'anapali,
Kā'anapali 667-2848, Maui
Marriott Resort, Kā'anapali
661-5425, Wailea Shopping
Village 874-0296
Emura Jewelers
49 Market St, Wailuku 244-0674
Fifth Avenue Mile
Dolphin Shopping Plaza 879-8122
Food Pantry
505 Front Street 661-5363/5364
Foodland
Ka'ahumanu Ctr 877-2808,
Lahaina Square Shopping Ctr
661-0975 (and other locations)
Fox Photo
Whalers Village 667-5494, 816
Front St, Lahaina 661-8895 (and
other locations)
Front Street Wholesale Eelskin
505 Front Street 661-5884
Gallery Kaanapali
Whalers Village 661-5571
Golden Eel Import Company
11 Market St, Wailuku 242-9613
Hasegawa General Store
PO Box 68, Hāna 248-8231
Hawaiian Etc
Kihei Town Ctr 879-2214
Health Spot
Kukui Mall, Kihei 879-0072
Herbs Etc
58 Central Ave, Wailuku 244-0420
Hilo Hattie's
1000 Limahana Pl., Lahaina
661-8457
The Hobby Habit
Maui Mall 871-6666

Honokowai Food Pantry
3636 HonoaPi'ilani Hwy, Nāpili
669-6208
Honsport
Kaahumanu Ctr 877-3954
Hopaco Stationers
Kaahumanu Ctr 871-8321
Ikeda's
71 Baldwin Ave, Pā'ia 579-9922,
Lahaina Shopping Ctr 661-3146,
81 Market St, Wailuku 244-5459
Island Camera & Gift Shops
Royal Lahaina Resort 661-8859,
Sheraton-Maui Hotel
661-4077/0031 x5191, Wailea
Shopping Village 879-3802
JR's Music Shop
Maui Mall 871-4585 (and other
locations)
**Jack Ackerman's The Original Maui
Divers**
Banyan Inn, Lahaina 661-0988
Jane's Shells & Craft
40 Baldwin Ave, Pā'ia 579-9288
Jenai's Hallmark Shop
Kaahumanu Ctr 877-6113
Judges' Beyond the Reef
Sugar Beach Resort, 145 N Kīhei
Rd, Kīhei 879-2979
Ka Honu Gift Gallery
Whalers Village 661-0173
Kaneshige Jewelers
Maui Mall 877-0116
Kapalua Gallery
123 Bay Dr., Kapalua 669-0202
Kapalua Shop
Kapalua Shops 669-4172
Kihei Drug
1881 S Kīhei Road 879-7290
Kramer's
Lahaina Cannery Ctr 661-5377,
Kaahumanu Ctr 871-8671
Kula Bay
120 Lahainaluna Rd, Lahaina
667-5852
Lady Di's
Rainbow Mall 879-7121

Lahaina Florist
Lahaina Shopping Ctr 661-0509/
8553
Lahaina Gallery
728 Front St, Lahaina 667-2152,
117 Lahainaluna Rd, Lahaina
661-0839
(and other locations)
Lahaina General Store
829 Front St, Lahaina 661-0944
Lahaina Printsellers
Whalers Village 667-7617,
Seamen's Hospital, Lahaina
667-7843, Wailea Shopping Village
879-1567
Lahaina Scrimshaw Factory
Whalers Village 661-4034,
Hyatt Regency Maui,
Kā'anapali 661-8286,
845A Front St, Lahaina 661-8820
(and other locations)
Lahaina Shoe & Luggage Repair
888 Waine'e St, Ste 111, Lahaina
661-3114
Lahaina Trader
709 Front St, Lahaina 661-8616
Leilani Gift Shop
Azeka Place 879-7506
Leisure Sundries
Maui Prince Hotel 879-9305
Liberty House
Kaahumanu Ctr 877-3361,
Azeka Place 879-7448
(and other locations)
Longhi The Shop
Kapalua Shops 669-5000
Longs Drug Stores
Maui Mall 877-0041,
Lahaina Cannery Ctr 667-4384
Mana Foods
49 Baldwin Ave, Pā'ia 579-8078
Mandalay Imports
Kapalua Shops 669-6170
Maui Clothing Co.
Azeka Place 879-7960, 658 Front
St, Lahaina 661-3062, Lahaina
Shopping Ctr 667-6090

Maui Crafts' Guild
43 Hāna Hwy, Pā'ia 579-9697
Maui Moorea Leather & Gifts
3639 Baldwin Ave, Makawao
572-0801
Maui Natural Foods
Maui Mall 877-3018
Maui on My Mind
Lahaina Cannery Ctr 667-5597
Maui's Best
Kaahumanu Ctr 877-2665, Maui
The Minit Stop
333 Dairy Rd, Kahului 871-7325,
745 E Main St, Wailuku 244-8003,
3310A Haleakalā Hwy, Makawao
572-6350
Mountain Fresh Market
3673 Baldwin Ave, Makawao
572-1488
Muumuu Factory to You
Lahaina Shopping Ctr 661-4278
Nagasako Super Market
Lahaina Shopping Ctr 661-0985/
0575
National Dollar Stores
2027 Main St, Wailuku 244-0855
Native By Judge's
Wailea Shopping Village 879-3075
Noda's Market
Kahului Shopping Ctr 877-3395
O'Rourke's Tourist Trap
The Wharf 661-0605, Kamaole
Shopping Ctr 879-0405, Azeka
Place 879-7055
Olowalu General Store
820 Olowalu Village 661-3774
Paradise Fruit Stand
1913 Kīhei Rd, Kīhei 879-1723
Paradise Lahaina
718 Front St, Lahaina 667-7547
Parrots of Maui
Lahaina Market Place
Pay 'n Save
200 E Kamehameha Ave, Kahului
877-3315
The Pearl Factory
Whalers Village 661-8042,
Lahaina Cannery Ctr 661-0115
(and other locations)

Pet Shop
Maui Mall 877-3040
Plantation Marketplace
Maui Tropical Plantation 244-7643
Provenance Gallery
Lahaina Market Place 667-6222
Pukalani Drugs
Pukalani Terrace Ctr 572-8244
Reyn's
Kapalua Shops 669-5260,
Lahaina Cannery Ctr 661-5356
Safeway Stores
170 E Kamehameha Ave, Kahului
877-3377, Lahaina Cannery Ctr
667-4392
Sea & Shell Gallery
Whalers Village 661-3730,
(and other locations)
Sears
Kaahumanu Ctr 877-2221
7-Eleven Food Stores
1847 S Kīhei Rd, Kīhei 879-7177,
111 Alamaha St, Kahului 877-4598
The Shell Stop!
Hāna Hwy
Shirokiya
Kaahumanu Ctr 877-5551
Silks Kaanapali, Ltd
Whalers Village 667-7133
Silversword Book and Card Store
Azeka Place 879-4373
Sir Wilfred's Coffee Tea Tobacco
Shop
Maui Mall 877-3711, Lahaina
Cannery Ctr 667-1941
South Pacific Gifts & Sundries
Hyatt Regency Kā'anapali,
Kā'anapali 661-3006/3388,
Westin Maui, Kā'anapali 661-0234
Star Markets
Maui Mall 877-3341, 1310 S Kīhei
Rd, Kīhei 879-5871
Su-Su's Boutique
Wailea Shopping Village 879-2623
Superwhale Children's Boutique
Whalers Village 661-0260,
Lahaina Cannery Ctr 661-3424
(and other locations)

T-Shirt Factory
Rainbow Mall 879-8066,
Maui Mall 877-0552,
21 N Market St, Wailuku
244-8215, Wailea Shopping
Village 879-7005
Tasaka Guri Guri
Maui Mall 871-4513
Tester's Shoe Repair
Old Kahului Store, 55 Ka'ahumanu
Ave, Kahului 877-7140
Tiger Lily
Old Kahului Store, 55 Ka'ahumanu
Ave, Kahului 871-2465
Toda Drugs
Kahului Shopping Ctr 871-4021
Traders
Royal Lahaina Resort 667-6016
Upcountry Protea Farm
Rte 1, PO Box 485F, Kula 878-2544
(Maui and interisland)
800 332-8233 (US mainland)
Valley Isle Pharmacy
2180 Main St, Wailuku 244-7252
Village Gallery
Lahaina Cannery Ctr 661-3280
The Village Gallery-Lahaina
120 Dickenson St, Lahaina
661-4402
Wailea Beach Shoppe
Stouffer Wailea Beach Resort
879-1411

Wailea 1 Hour Photo
3750 Wailea Alanui Rd, Kihei
879-7577
Wailea Pantry
3750 Wailea Alanui Rd #B-1, Kihei
879-3044
Waldenbooks
Kaahumanu Ctr 871-6112,
Kukui Mall 874-3688,
Lahaina Cannery Ctr 667-6172,
Maui Mall 877-0181,
Whalers Village 661-8638
Westside Natural Foods
136 Dickenson St, Lahaina
667-2855
**Whaler's Book Shoppe & Coffee
House**
The Wharf 667-9544
Whaler's Chest
Royal Lahaina Resort 667-9180
Whalers General Store
505 Front Street 661-3504,
180 Dickenson Street 661-4663,
101 N. Kihei Road 879-7465,
2463 S. Kihei Rd #A11 879-8670,
5425D Lower Honoapiilani Rd
669-6773,
Pioneer Inn, Lahaina 661-8871,
Kukui Mall, Kihei 879-7499
Woolworth
Maui Mall 877-3934

HAWAIIAN WORDLIST

T hese words are likely to be seen or heard by anyone visiting these islands. Some may be seen without the markings that alter pronunciation (and meaning), as explained in the INTRODUCTION. In the pronunciation guides given here, typical English syllables which most closely approximate the Hawaiian vowel sounds are used; a precise rendition would require long and complex explanations. The *'okina* [glottal stop], creating the hard sound, has been retained to show where adjacent vowels should not slide from one to the other; syllables with elongated vowels are written twice, and stress is indicated by capitalization.

a'ā [AH-'AH] a rough, crumbly type of lava
aikāne [aye-KAH-neh] friend
akamai [ah-kah-my-ee] smart, wise, on the ball
ali'i [ah-LEE-'ee] chief, nobility
aloha [ah-LO-ha] love, greetings, hello, good-bye
aloha a nui loa [ah-LO-ha ah NOO-ee LO-ah] much love
auē, auwē [ah-oo-EH-EH] alas!, oh dear!, too bad!, goodness!
'awa [AH-vah] traditional Polynesian drink wrung from the roots of the pepper plant (kava)
hana hou [hah-nah HO-oo] encore, do it again
hanohano [hah-no-HAH-no] distinguished, magnificent
haole [HAH-oh-leh] originally foreigner; now Caucasian
hapa [HAH-pa] half, part
hapa-haole [HAH-pa HAH-oh-leh] half Caucasian
Hau'oli Makahiki Hou [ha-oo-'oh-lee mah-ka-hee-kee ho-oo] Hawaiian translation of Happy New Year (now used, but not a traditional greeting)
haupia [ha-oo-PEE-ah] coconut pudding
heiau [HEH-ee-ah-oo] ancient Hawaiian place of worship
hele [HEH-leh] go, walk around
holoholo [ho-lo-HO-lo] to visit about, make the rounds
holokū [ho-LO-koo] a fitted, ankle-length dress, sometimes with train
ho'olaule'a [ho-'oh-lah-oo-LAY-'ah] celebration
hui [HOO-ee] club, association
hukilau [HOO-kee-lah-oo] community net-fishing party
hula [HOO-lah] Hawaiian dance
huli [HOO-lee] turn over, turn around
humuhumunukunukuāpua'a [hoo-moo-hoo-moo-noo-koo-noo-koo-ah-poo-AH-'ah] Hawai'i's State Fish; a small triggerfish famous for its long name
iki [EE-kee] little (size)
imu [EE-moo] ground oven
imua [ee-MOO-ah] forward, onward
kāhili [kah-ah-HEE-lee] a royal feathered standard
kahuna [kah-HOO-nah] priest, expert
kai [KY-ee] sea, sea water
kālā [KAH-lah] money (literally dollar)
kama'āina [kah-mah-AYE-nah] native born, longtime Hawai'i resident, old established family

kanaka [kah-NAH-kah] originally 'man' or person; now a native Hawaiian
kāne [KAH-neh] boy, man, husband
kapa [KAH-pah] tapa cloth (made from mulberry bark)
kapakahi [kah-pah-KAH-hee] crooked, lopsided
kapu [KAH-poo] forbidden, sacred, taboo, keep out
kaukau [KAH-oo-kah-oo] food
keiki [KAY-kee] child
kiawe [kee-AH-vay] mesquite tree
kōkua [ko-KOO-ah] help, assistance, aid
kona [KO-nah] winds 'that blow against the trades', lee side of an island
kukui [koo-KOO-ee] candlenut tree
kumu [KOO-moo] teacher
lānai [lah-NY-ee] porch, terrace, veranda
lani [LAH-nee] heaven, heavenly, sky
lauhala [lah-oo-HAH-lah] leaf of the pandanus tree (for weaving)
laulau [LAH-oo-lah-oo] bundled food in ti leaves
lei [LAY-ee] garland of flowers, shells or feathers, wreath
liliko'i [lee-lee-KOH-ee] passion fruit
loa [LO-ah] long
lomi [LO-mee] rub, press, massage, type of raw salmon (usually lomilomi)
lua [LOO-ah] toilet, restroom
lū'au [LOO-'ah-oo] feast, party, taro leaf
mahalo [mah-HAH-loh] thank you
mahimahi [mah-hee-MAH-hee] dorado or dolphin fish
māhū [MAH-hoo] gay, homosexual
makai [mah-KY-ee] toward the sea
make [MAH-keh] dead
makule [mah-KOO-leh] elderly, old (of people)
malihini [mah-lee-HEE-nee] newcomer, visitor
malo [MAH-lo] man's loincloth
mauka [MAH-oo-ka] toward the mountains, inland
mauna [MAH-oo-nah] mountain
Mele Kalikimaka [meh-leh kah-lee-kee-MAH-ka] Merry Christmas
Menehune [meh-neh-HOO-neh] legendary race of dwarfs
moemoe [mo-eh-MO-eh] sleep
mu'umu'u [moo-'oo-moo-'oo] long or short loose-fitting dress
nui [NOO-ee] big
'ohana [oh-HAH-nah] family, extended family
'ōkole [oh-oh-KO-lay] buttocks, bottom, rear
'ōkole maluna [oh-oh-ko-lay-mah-LOO-nah] Hawaiian translation of 'bottoms up' (a bit crude)
'ono [OH-no] delicious
'ōpū [OH-OH-POO-OO] abdomen, stomach
pakalōlō [pah-kah-LO-lo] marijuana
Pākē [PAH-keh] Chinese
pali [PAH-lee] cliff, precipice; *the* Pali=the Nu'uanu Pali
paniolo [pah-nee-OH-lo] cowboy
pau [PA-oo] finished, done
pau hana [pa-oo HAH-nah] finish work
pāhoehoe [pah-ho-eh-HO-eh] type of lava with smooth or ropy surface

pīkake [pee-KAH-keh] jasmine flower, named after 'peacock'
poi [POY] pasty food made from pounded taro
puka [POO-kah] hole, door
pūpū [POO-poo] hors d'oeuvres (literally 'shells')
tūtū [TOO-TOO] grandmother, affectionate term for old people—relatives or friends—of grandparents' generation (According to the rules of language set down by the missionaries, there is no 't' in the Hawaiian language, but hardly anyone ever says kūkū.)
'uku [OO-koo] fleas, head lice
'ukulele [oo-koo-LAY-leh] small, stringed instrument from Portugal
wahine [va-HEE-neh, wah-HEE-neh] girl, woman, wife
wikiwiki [wee-kee-WEE-kee] fast, in a hurry, quickly

PIDGIN ENGLISH WORDLIST

The pronunciation of pidgin is self-evident, and its spelling is phonic rather than fixed. In most cases, the derivation is also obvious. The lilt that is peculiar to this local lingo cannot be adequately described; it must be heard. This list is given as a guide to listening only. Trying to speak pidgin involves the risk of inadvertently saying something offensive or insulting. Everyone who speaks pidgin also understands correctly spoken English.

an den? So? What next? What else? [and then]
any kine anything [any kind]
ass right you are correct [that's right]
bambucha big
bambula big
beef fight
blalah heavy set, Hawaiian man, may be looking for a fight
bradah friend [brother]
brah short for bradah
buggah guy, friend, pest
bumbye after awhile, [by and by]
bummahs too bad, disappointed expression [bummer]
cockaroach rip off, steal, confiscate
cool head main ting keep calm, relax
da the
da kine anything being discussed, used as either noun or verb when the speaker can't think of the right word
dat that
dem them, guys, folks
eh? you know, do you understand?; also used at the beginning of a statement
garans guaranteed, for sure
geevum go for it! [give them]
grind eat
grinds food
had it destroyed, wrecked

haaah? what? I didn't hear you
haolefied like a haole
hele on go, leave, 'with it', 'hip'
high mucka mucka arrogant, conceited, elite
ho! exclamation used before a strong statement
how you figga? how do you figure that, makes no sense
howzit hi, hello, how are you doing, what's happening [how is it]
junk lousy, terrible
kay den okay then, fine
li'dat like that, short cut for lengthy explanation
li'dis like this
humbug trouble, bother
make 'A' make a fool of yourself [make ass]
make house make yourself at home, act like you own the place
mama-san local Japanese equivalent of 'mom' at 'mom and pop' stores
Maui wowie potent marijuana (from Maui)
minors no big thing, minor
mo' more
mo' bettah better, good stuff
moke heavy set Hawaiian male, often looking for a fight
nah just kidding (often **nah, nah, nah**)
no can cannot, I can't do it
o' wot? (added on to most questions, usually when the speaker is fed up) [or what]
poi dog mutt, person made up of many ethnic mixtures
Popolo black, Negro
shahkbait white-skinned, pale [shark bait]
shaka all right, great, well done, perfect, okay, right on
sleepahs flip flops, thongs [slippers]
stink eye dirty look, evil eye
talk story rap, shoot the breeze, gossip
tanks eh? thank you
tita heavy set Hawaiian woman, may be looking for a fight [sister]
try used at beginning of a command
we go let's leave
yeah? added on to end of sentences
yeah yeah yeah yeah yes, all right, shut up

RECOMMENDED READING

There are countless books—of varying quality and accuracy—detailing the many aspects of Hawaiian history and culture, both ancient and modern. It has been impossible to detail any of these fascinating areas in a guide-book small enough to be handy. We recommend the following:

Atlas of Hawaii, **by the Department of Geography, University of Hawai'i,** University of Hawai'i Press, 1983. This book provides text on Hawai'i's natural environment, culture and economy along with maps.

The Beaches of Maui County, **by John R. K. Clark,** University of Hawai'i Press, 1980. A complete guide to the beaches of Maui, Moloka'i, Lāna'i and Kaho'olawe, with maps, photographs, safety rules, local history and beach lore.

Bird Life in Hawaii, **by Andrew J. Berger,** Island Heritage, 1987. This fascinating story of the bird life of Hawai'i begins with the formation of the Hawaiian Islands and the arrival of the first birds through subsequent immigrations of exotic birds, including species which have become rare and endangered, each illustrated in full color accompanied by text written by the world's leading authority on Hawaiian birds.

The Divers' Guide to Hawaii, **by Chuck Thorne and Lou Zitnik,** Hawaii Divers' Guide Press, 1984. Useful guide which includes black and white maps and descriptions of dive sites on Maui.

Entertaining Island Style, **by Lavonne Tollerud and Barbara Gray,** Island Heritage, 1987. Menu planning is made simple in this colorful book. From lu'au and beach parties to elegant Hawaiian suppers, there are many ideas for entertaining.

Favorite Recipes from Hawaii, **by Lavonne Tollerud and Barbara Gray,** Island Heritage, 1987. A collection of Hawai'i's most popular recipes. It includes Hawaiian cocktails, hors d'oeuvres, soups, salads, breads, main dishes, condiments, rice and noodles, vegetables and desserts.

Flowers of Hawaii, **photography by Allan Seiden and Loye Gutherie,** Island Heritage, 1987. A beautifully-photographed guide to Hawai'i's colorful flowers, such as hibiscus, orchids and lilies, and their origins.

A Guide to Hawaiian Marine Life, **by Les Matsuura,** Island Heritage, 1987. Written by a marine educator at the Waikīkī Aquarium, this guide highlights the marine life in Hawai'i through description and color photographs.

Hawaii, **by James Michener,** Random, 1959. A novel about Hawai'i from its geological birth to the present, by this renowned author.

Hawaii: The Aloha State, **by Allan Seiden,** Island Heritage, 1987. Visit exciting Waikīkī, colorful Lahaina, majestic Waimea Canyon, historic Kona—all the Hawaiian islands are brought to life in this beautifully-photographed book.

Hawaii: A History, by Ralph S. Kuykendall, Prentice, 1961. A good and readable overall history of Hawai'i from the first Polynesian voyages to statehood.

Hawaii: An Uncommon History, by Ed Joesting, W.W. Norton & Co., 1978. This book tells of the bicentennial history of the state in a series of episodes written in depth.

Hawaii's Best Hiking Trails, by Robert Smith, Wilderness Press, 1985. Ninety-three of the best hiking trails on O'ahu, Kaua'i, Maui, the Big Island, Lāna'i and Moloka'i including descriptions on how to get there and what you'll see, both beside the trail and in panoramic views.

Hawaiian Antiquities, by David Malo, Bishop Museum Press, 1951. Completed in 1839, this text shows Hawaiian culture and society in Pre-Christian times. Plants, birds, weapons, tools, origin of the Hawaiians, *ali'i,* morality and belief, surfing and other activities are focused on. Originally written in Malo's native language, Hawaiian, it shows patterns of Hawaiian thought.

168

Hawaiian Dictionary, by Mary Kawena Pukui and Samuel H. Elbert, University of Hawai'i Press, 1986. Hawaiian-English, English-Hawaiian dictionary, regarded as the definitive reference for Hawaiian vocabulary. It contains folklore, poetry and ethnology compiled by the leading authorities of Hawaiiana and Polynesian languages.

Hiking Maui, by Robert Smith, Wilderness Press, 1984. This accurate guidebook lists hiking trails on Maui, with descriptions of the route, highlights, rating of difficulty, driving instructions, distance and average hiking time.

The Illustrated Atlas of Hawaii, by Gavan Daws, O.A. Bushnell & Andrew Berger, Island Heritage, 1987. Illustrations of the Hawaiian island chain, native plants, birds and fish by Joseph Feher with a concise history.

The Island of Lanai: A Survey of Native Culture, by Kenneth P. Emory, Bishop Museum Press, 1969. The only writing of its kind, this book focuses on archaeology and anthropology of Lāna'i, and the history, customs, traditions and original genealogy of the first inhabitants of the island. Sketches and photos of *heiau*s also included.

The Journal of Prince Alexander Liholiho, Jacob Adler, ed., University of Hawai'i Press, 1967. Young Alexander Liholiho and his brother Lot visited the United States, England and France on a diplomatic mission with Dr Judd. This diary records the impressions of the future king.

Ka Po'e Kahiko: The People of the Old, by Samuel M. Kamakau, Bishop Museum Press, 1987. This book and its companion, *The Works of the People of Old: Na Hana a ka Po'e Kahiko* are based on a series of articles written for the Hawaiian language newspaper *Ke Au 'Oko'a* in 1868 and 1870 designed to preserve Hawaiian culture that had been disappearing in the nineteenth century.

Kaaawa: A Novel About Hawaii in the 1850s, by Oswald Bushnell, University of Hawai'i Press, 1972. An historical novel set on O'ahu about the missionary period.

Ka'ahumanu: Molder of Change, by Jane Silverman, Friends of the Judiciary History Center of Hawaii, 1987. A biography of the most powerful woman in Hawaiian history and the vast changes she wrought in the social and political life of the kingdom she ruled.

Kahuna La'au Lapa'au: The Practice of Hawaiian Herbal Medicine, by June Gutmanis, Island Heritage, 1987. Authoritative and definitive work on Hawaiian herbs and the secrets of Hawaiian herbal medicine with colorful illustrations.

Kalakaua: Hawaii's Last King, by Kristin Zambucka, Mana Publishing Co. and Marvin/Richard Enterprises, Inc., 1983. This pictorial biography with more than 180 old photographs recounts the colorful reign of Hawai'i's last king. Author/artist Zambucka has an extensive background in studies of the Pacific area and its peoples.

The Kumulipo: A Hawaiian Creation Chant, Martha Warren Beckwith, ed., University of Hawai'i Press, 1972. Beckwith translates and annotates this authentic work of primitive literature, which remains one of the primary sources on Hawaiian mythology, political structure and way of life.

Maui: An Introduction, by Allan Seiden, Island Heritage, 1985. This brief book shows a stunning combination of photographs from different sections of Maui.

Maui The Valley Isle, by Allan Seiden, Island Heritage, 1986. This work contains photographs, history, tales and other information about Maui and its people.

Māui: The Demigod, by Steven Goldsberry, Poseidon Press, 1984. This work about a universal figure in Polynesian folktales is remarkable for its utter originality and beauty of its language. The story is wise and funny, erotic and terrifying, and filled with humanity, folly and fate.

Molokai, by Oswald Bushnell, World Publishing Company, 1963. A novel about a group of people sent to a leper colony on Moloka'i and the shocking details of their lives.

Myths and Legends of Hawaii, by W.A. Westervelt, Mutual Publishing Co., 1987. A broadly inclusive one volume collection of folklore by this leading authority including the great prehistoric Māui, Hina, Pele and her fiery family, and a dozen other heroic beings, human or ghostly.

Na Pule Kahiko: Ancient Hawaiian Prayers, by June Gutmanis, Editions Limited, 1983. This collection of traditional Hawaiian prayers, in both Hawaiian and English, is annotated with details about the contexts in which these prayers, and prayers in general, were used in the lives of ancient Hawaiians.

Niihau Shell Leis, by Linda Paik Moriarty, University of Hawai'i Press, 1986. An expert documentation of the traditions of this unique art, richly illustrated with color photographs of the many varieties of this rare and precious, gem-quality shell, and based on personal interviews with Ni'ihau women who are actively engaged in this ancient craft.

Notable Women of Hawaii, **Barbara Bennett Peterson, ed.,** University of Hawai'i Press, 1984. A biographical reference work documenting women's contributions to the history of the Hawaiian Islands.

An Ocean in Mind, **by Will Kyselka,** University of Hawai'i Press, 1987. The extraordinary story of a 6000-mile trip from Hawai'i to Tahiti and back, the 1980 voyage of the *Hōkūle'a,* without the use of modern navigational aid. Navigator Nainoa Thompson, of Hawaiian descent, studied the stars, winds and currents to explore his Polynesian past.

The Peopling of Hawaii, **by Eleanor C. Nordyke,** University of Hawai'i Press, 1977. A review of Hawai'i's people and the effects of population growth on an island community.

Place Names of Hawaii, **by Mary Kawena Pukui, Samuel H. Elbert & Esther T. Mookini,** University of Hawai'i Press, 1974. Place names listed with pronunciation and translation where known. Includes names of valleys, streams, mountains, land sections, surfing areas, towns, villages and Honolulu streets and buildings. Pukui and Elbert also compiled the *Hawaiian Dictionary.* Mookini has taught the Hawaiian language at the University of Hawai'i.

Princess Kaiulani: Last Hope of Hawaii's Monarchy, **by Kristin Zambucka,** Mana Publishing Co., 1982. Pictorial biography of Hawai'i's beautiful and tragic princess. Niece of Queen Lili'uokalani, Hawai'i's last reigning monarch, Princess Ka'iulani, was next in the line of succession to the throne.

Pua Nani, **by Jeri Bostwick, photographs by Douglas Peebles,** Mutual Publishing, 1987. Stunning color photography of the myriad blossoms—both native and introduced—that festoon these islands with their glorious hues and intricate structures.

The Return of Lono, **by Oswald Bushnell,** University of Hawai'i Press, 1971. A fictional reconstruction of the discovery of the Hawaiian Islands by Captain Cook.

Shoal of Time, **by Gavan Daws,** University of Hawai'i Press, 1974. An excellent and authoritative history of Hawai'i from earliest times to statehood, 1959.

Sweet Voices of Lahaina, The Story of Maui's Fabulous Farden Family, **by Mary C. Richards,** Island Heritage Publishing, 1990. A warm, charming and informative biography of Hawaii's first family of music.

Tropical Drinks and Pupus from Hawaii, **by Lavonne Tollerud and Barbara Gray,** Island Heritage, 1987. Delicious island cocktails and fruit drinks are complemented with a wide range of Hawaiian style hors d'oeuvres.

Under a Maui Sun, A Celebration of the Island of Maui, **by Penny Pence Smith,** Island Heritage Publishing, 1989. An extraordinarily beautiful photographic exploration of today's Maui. More than 200 images from Hawaii's finest photographers, accompanied by an essay on the history and culture of the island.

INDEX

172

PHOTO CREDITS:

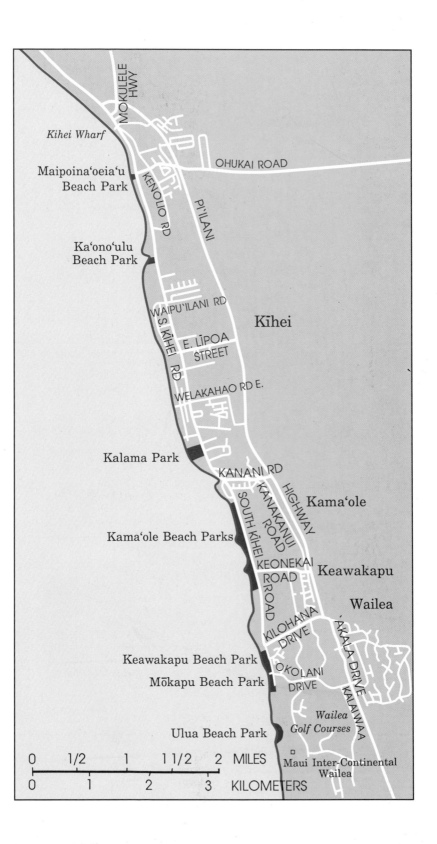

MOKULELE HWY

Kihei Wharf

Maipoina'oeia'u
Beach Park

OHUKAI ROAD

KENOLIO RD

PI'ILANI

Ka'ono'ulu
Beach Park

WAIPU'ILANI RD

S. KIHEI RD

Kīhei

E. LĪPOA
STREET

WELAKAHAO RD E.

Kalama Park

KANANI RD

HIGHWAY

KANAKANUI ROAD

Kama'ole

Kama'ole Beach Parks

SOUTH KIHEI ROAD

KEONEKAI
ROAD

Keawakapu

KILOHANA DRIVE

Wailea

'AKALA DRIVE

Keawakapu Beach Park

'OKOLANI
DRIVE

KALAWAA

Mōkapu Beach Park

*Wailea
Golf Courses*

Ulua Beach Park

| 0 | 1/2 | 1 | 1 1/2 | 2 | MILES |

| 0 | 1 | 2 | 3 | KILOMETERS |

Maui Inter-Continental
Wailea

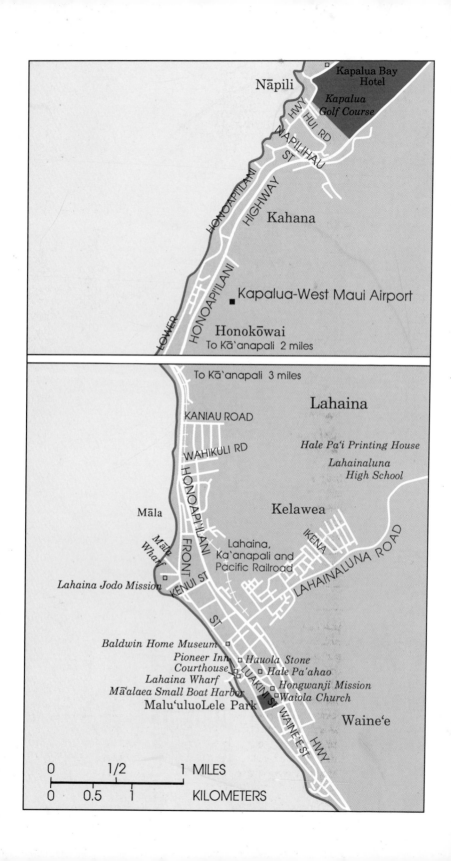

Nāpili

Kapalua Bay
Hotel

*Kapalua
Golf Course*

HWY HUI RD

NAPILIHAU ST

HONOAPI'ILANI HIGHWAY

Kahana

LOWER HONOAPI'ILANI

■ Kapalua-West Maui Airport

Honokōwai
To Kā'anapali 2 miles

To Kā'anapali 3 miles

Lahaina

KANIAU ROAD

WAHIKULI RD

Hale Pa'i Printing House

*Lahainaluna
High School*

HONOAPI'ILANI

Māla

Kelawea

*Māla
Wharf*

IKENA

LAHAINALUNA ROAD

Lahaina Jodo Mission

FRONT

KENUI ST

Lahaina,
Ka'anapali and
Pacific Railroad

ST

Baldwin Home Museum

Pioneer Inn   ☐ *Hauola Stone*
Courthouse   ☐ *Hale Pa'ahao*
Lahaina Wharf   ☐ *Hongwanji Mission*
Mā'alaea Small Boat Harbor   ☐ *Waiola Church*

LUAKINI ST

Malu'uluoLele Park

WAINE'E ST

HWY

Waine'e

0	1/2	1 MILES
0	0.5	1 KILOMETERS